Dear Richard,
Hope you enjoy your
1st Christmas with us 2007
lots of love
Louise + Wayne
xxxxx

Bile

ALBUM

The Books of Albion

The Books of Albion

The Collected Writings of

Peter Doherty

'A young man's journey over the last seven or eight years. In and out of consciousness, in and out of Pentonville, in and out of several hearts, homes and hostels . . . I was always a candid sort of fellow when it came to putting ink on to paper. There's a lot of honesty in there . . . a few gems of the old Irish philosophy . . . definitely a lot of sadness – a few attempts at thinly disguised fiction.'

Peter Doherty

I'd dedicate these writings
to my true love. Meh

Peter Doherty
London May 2007.

Let this be an itinerary, if only a pop metaphysical one...

10th February 1999

Southbound on the Northern Line towards the inaugural Paradigm Poets parade down at the Poetry Place in Covent Garden. John Citizen, Victoria Mocely (yeah, related) et al will be gagging and groaning before a cluster of lucky souls, although my own role in events is somewhat unclear. I am an official Paradigm Poet, and attended the Holland Park photo shoot some weeks back. Tonight I shall be asked to perform. Later.

London chronicles:

A verve reprise winds & spirals out of the 4 speakers in the 70's jag speeding down the Mile End Road. A midnight meeting at the Prince Charles. What does Morrissey's sister do, I wonder? German wants a pork-pie hat. Who will sell me a lie?

An old music hall sing along plink plonked out on an old ivory key joanna during the saddest, smokiest lock-in in a Spitalfields pub they forgot to buy-out, gut-out & refurbish for a new targeted consumer. A morning meeting in a closed park. Where is the next Prime Minister? French wants new shoes. Who will buy?

Stationary at a café table.

The launch of Paradigm Poets is not until Friday - much to my embarrassment. Still - better two days early than a second late, to adapt my mothers philosophy. Fran popped in very briefly. He has a screen test for Nickelodeon next week, and a plan for him & I to run poetry unplugged if and when Herr Citizen chooses to rest from his duties.

The Albion is still on course, though the route is annoyingly prone to be more akin to a Sid James Mystery Tour than a plain-sailing maiden voyage. Tension on ship as ever, but more body mass to absorb & ease it. Steve sings. Justin plays bass. Carlos & I stoke the furnace. For now this is the format. A 2-track demo has been cut and the word must now be spread. Instruments are being bought, new songs being written. I would of course not hesitate to describe myself as the ideal frontman for the songs - not least because they are mostly written with the blood of my heart - but I do relish the opportunity of watching Steve perform live from close quarters. I have plenty of stage to myself with the performance poetry malarkey, which is providing a great deal of interest at the moment. Adv, drunk & gloriously shameful at the Foundry, has assured me that I am to host the Sunday night poetry sessions whilst he tours. Last week, I dragged Francesca along to the low-lit wooden Bohemian haven bar/workshop/gallery as I rattled off a few oldies & played some songs. Wasn't quite carried shoulder high from the stage but I was pleased with the reception.

Friday should prove interesting.

my life is a sequel,
my love a trailer.
She wont watch read or
buy me – so
I shall be forced to
impail her .....

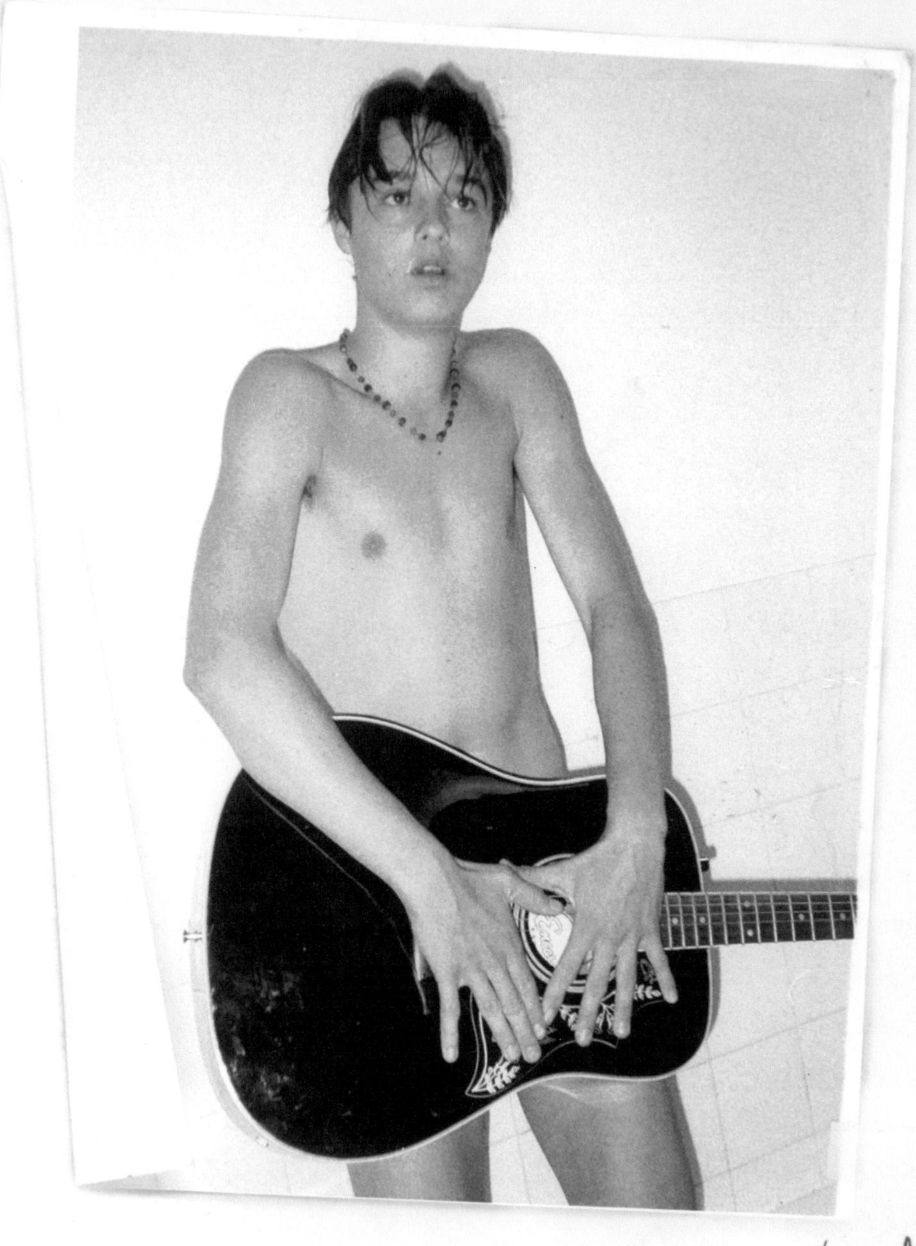

Woe and blast in response to the ~~pe~~ perennial problem
of housing. Such is the state of the present that
I can no longer think of returning to 236 Camden
Road without offering up a plea that everyone I
know has been temporarily deprived of limbs - thus
rendering them little hope of piling in, crashing
down, bleeding me dry of time and patience.
without any clue as to the basics of self-sufficiency,
Carlos is a slight burden - but still a richly talented
and quite noble old stick who goes well out of his way
not to prise anything out my weak grasp. Simply, I

require a cheap, spacious room somewhere central. Perhaps an advertisement in some suitable publication might not go amiss. 'POET, YOUNG & BUSY, SEEKS CHEAP, SPACIOUS ROOMS SOMEWHERE CENTRAL / WEST / NORTH LONDON. EXCELLENT REFERENCES AVAILABLE.'

---

*'Film Producer requires story readers to synopsize books at home. CV to Box TLS 867 Admiral House 66-68 East Smithfield London E1 9XY

Recent films seen: [Nil by Mouth], [O! Lucky Man], [The last Days of Disco], [Velvet Goldmine] [My Fair Lady], [Funny Face]

The first is a very absorbing look at a dysfunctional as they come South London family. Funny & frightening & wonderfully acted & filmed. A film that exists with an autonomy ~~[illegible]~~ and would probably stick 2 fingers up at anyone who claimed to either love or loathe it. It is hard to write about a film that is so ~~[illegible]~~ convincing. O! Lucky Man is Lindsay Anderson's classic psychedelic romp through 60's English consciousness. Bawdy, bathetic & brilliant clothes colours & accents. Arthur Lowe playing black with boot polish, Malcolm McDowell perched on a ledge quoting Hamlet - trying to convince a suicidal housewife that life is worth .... the 3 hour showpiece of surreality, Alan Price songs and an England close-up that will never be seen again. The last days of disco is dire - as is the mind-numbingly stale 'Velvet Goldmine'. A wanky pastiche of the 70's glam era - forbidden to use any Bowie songs the creators have a mountain to climb from the start: they shouldn't have left base-camp. Redeeming features include cameos by Eddie Izzard, Donna from Elastica & the surprisingly charismatic Placebo, but generally the chance to capture the sleazy aesthetically super-charged splendour of that era (in all its sexual lushness & intoxicated head-fuck freakiness) has still not been grabbed at by deserving hands.

One wonders if the Britpop era will era be looked back on with any affection. I sincerely doubt it. Spending some time with the likes of Johnny 'Menswear' & Sheila Chesterton (ex-Elastica), many heroes of the day are now washed up on a desert island of ill-luck & obscurity. Everyone agrees that Blur & Supergrass have written their best stuff in their later albums – and the 2 most coveted bands of ~~the~~ the 90's era (Radiohead & The Verve) had nothing to do with Britpop. Pulp is a little less clear-cut. They excelled – and probably came to define Britpop – with the 'Common People' performance at Glasto. Not so much with the song (a song with no merit compared to much earlier, and indeed much more recent work), but with their capacity to gather the attention of all who watched the launch of jumped on and fell off the bandwagon.

Echobelly, Sleeper, Blur, Supergrass, Pulp & Oasis, Elastica, Bluetone, Cast even Dodgy – these bands many people no longer even admire as Ground Zero/333/Vibe Bar vibes penetrate. Guitars are not hip, not quite, not quite yet again. It was not a ~~music akin~~ movement akin to Baggy, Mod, Punk or Goth or anything. It was just pop that sounded similar & lots of hair, adidas, gigging, Fred Perry & denim flares. Some of those bands listed are quite simply laughable. They were adored at the time. Christ what I wouldn't give to live through an era whose pop music, youth culture, social change & some intelligent ideals went arm in harm, tongue on tongue together. Did one ever exist? Can I ever create one? Do I need anything more than energy & a photocopier. Enough rambling. I want to create a band that people will be sorry to miss, and obliged to adore. The Smiths had a special power. As did the Roses, the Jam and, according to taste, many others. Something very English – imagine having melody, range, emotion, something to say and wear that attracts, interests and informs even instructs those that buy your records & mouth your words.

I want to have a crack before I outgrow this youthful urge to be worshipped, this need to fill a ladder on English pop's evolutionary chart. I have a band (almost) and the spirit of the Albion enthuses it. A not quite ideal C.D has been cut, and a live performance seems fairly imminent. I want somebody, somewhere to feel it in his best interest to defend himself (at the threat of violence) in his belief that 'The Libertines' (or whatever we call ourselves) are perfection & beauty personified.

---

cognition: Action or faculty of knowing, perceiving, conceiving, as opposed to emotion and volition. A perception.

'Boisson fade et mélancholique' Balzac's tea.

[one side] On one side is the flexing muscle of 'strength'. In particular, the strength to maintain those troublesome pillars that many claim prop up the self – principles. All the promises I have made, the vows uttered in moments of such profundity I dare not speak of my life without them easing into play – without their memories shouting for affectionate recollection and serious heartfelt reassertions of trust, loyalty, eternity & truth. If ties loosen am I not guilty of the worst form of betrayal: the betrayal of ones own principles.

warm nights in suicidal gardens, tussles in the street, a lack of new-inspired songs or sonnets: such are the moments – many are the moments that deliberation and pensive pontification become my minds set agenda.

The strength to draw strength from this testing of my strength – this is what I occassionally relish. Are these occassions enough? strained relations.

[the other] On the other I have a vision of a healthy, creative life as whatever service to humanity calls me. My wells are deep, my eyes are keen and my heart is full of hope, love & passion. My stomach is full of ambition & a few guts. My head is full of brain and my head full of hair. What more might I ask of a creator. Fertility, felicity and fire. Ideally, in the short term, success as a popstar, a performance poet and a musician is my inclination.

'If you've lost your faith in Love & music, the end won't be long ... & if it's gone for you then I too may lose it, and that would be wrong. I've tried so hard to keep myself from falling back into my bad old ways & it chars my heart to always hear you calling, calling for the good old days ... because there were no good old days ... these are the good old days. Arcadia's dream has fallen through, but I feel no remorse – she was born outside the light in a graveyard blue. I was born up in the north ... so.

A cup of tea, Charley Dean
to ease your miseries
Your war, your family,
Your new flat in Kilburn - been
there since 73,
since 83, on your own
The England designed by you
can't be found,
and you feel so much on your own
The England life gave to you,
is long gone away
and you have never felt so ready
to leave\and look for it.
So out you go

The Stoned Englishman

The smell of the liniment,
the clang of the ball
on the metal of the tin
roof of the supporters
club roof.

what about that sight on platform 2 Southbound.
Heaving, thronging, heavy the platform with white
English males. Beefy white English males. Football
crowd. There went I once upon a youth. Today
in my Levi-Strauss Sta-prests, black laceless Ben
Shermans, full length brown leather jacket, 70's zip-up
cardigan, black leather briefcase & beatles bob hair,
I'd be lucky get to the ground without having at
least one occassion to grose my teeth.
The aggressive tension in the air was mature & hard
with time. No-one wears colours - only the kids & the
cunts & the anoraks - everyone knows that now.

The Streets of Longing

cont from →

Freddy was a fusion. He said he was 'I'm a fusion' he'd grin, slyly.* And it was amazing enough for a while, but all the while Freddy was losing touch with what he could have been, or should have been. King.

I hadn't known him at school, he was a little bit older, a bit cool, but we cemented our funny friendship in that wilderness between leaving that school & first real jobs

Freddy said that this wilderness should ideally last a lifetime.

Now he appears lost for a lifetime – gone into ~~the river or into a~~ some river of ~~some~~ one of his minds.

He couldn't let go – where is taking you, I would ask, my lips ~~to~~ pressed white together. He fell from the sky, never to land – never a sound: just words 'Every blues song in the world has the answer – I'll tell you in the morning.

The boy stood on the burning deck
It was halfpast nine on Friday
His braces snapped his trouser fell
He wasn't very tidy

Baring his straight white teeth, letting me note down the results of his experimentation, his fusions.

Freddy was a fusion.
The rags around his minds were torn patchwork quilts of youth cults, forgotten grooves, visions and unprintable politics, with the odd bloody bandage of High Art and an aesthetic to grind away the gap between deep black dub & Oscar Wilde. Because Freddy was a deep black Oscar - his life was his gift, his bomber jacket buttonhole was his anarchy - Black as heaven he was and he lived next to my terrible Auntie Lucy 2 floors up on the White City Estate, in a tenement that reclaimed the colonies for the Hammersmith & Fulham benefits agency. From the window of the khazi you could see QPR's ground, and for ~~reasons~~ not yet understood Freddy ~~would~~, as a child would ~~crouch~~ squat on the ~~ss~~ sill groaning with the roars from the loft.

Freddy was a fusion. His ~~politics~~ beliefs a jamboree, a carnival of post everything neo nothing or next to nothing thought. He'd talk about Plato & Malcolm X, The French Revolution & Welsh devolution Notting Hill Riots, Chas & Dave & Marx & Earl Spencer He knew a lot about nothing in particular, & a little of the particulars about lots of things.

Freddy was a fusion - he took me to church, took me joyriding - speeding out of our ears up the A40 - he'd whisper 'All's Quiet On The Western Avenue' not audible above the Val Doonican or the Speed Garage - the sweat & sour smoke of his perennial pipe pumping out the ~~herbal~~ perfume - clouding, rearranging - brains ..... OLD HOLBORN & HONOLOLOU HERBS

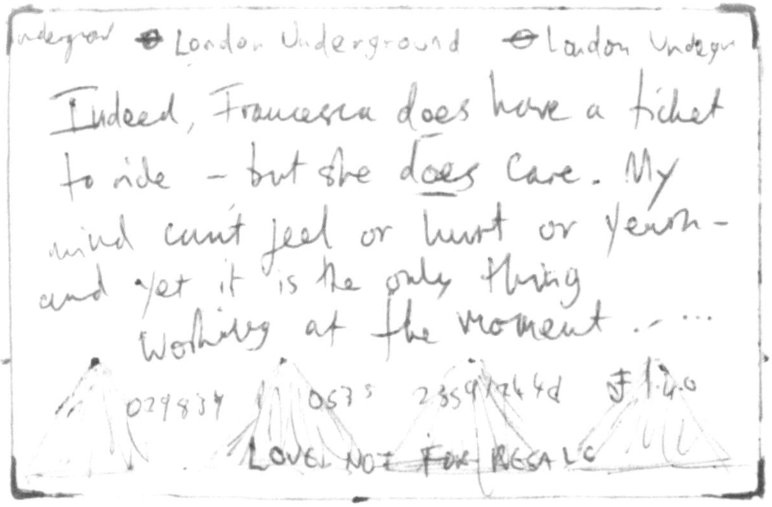
ndegrou ⊖ London Underground ⊖ London Undergr
Indeed, Francesca does have a ticket to ride – but she does care. My mind can't feel or hurt or yearn – and yet it is the only thing working at the moment . . . ...
029837 0675 2359 744d £1.40
LOVE NOT FOR RESALE

I: I must at all costs recover the £350 from dear lunatic Justin

II: I must make a concerted effort never to trust entirely another human being, family excepted

III: I must strive to improve my diet. Fruit, vegetables, brown bread & water. My addiction to fried chicken has become horrifyingly close to Tabloid material.

IV: I must try to surround myself with a few more stable & sane characters, lest I allow the worst in me to be dragged out and pampered by the puff pads of peers untamed

V: I must purchase a black bowler hat.

She said 'Sheffield's a special place'

Madness

Imagine being in a straight-jacket – the freedom allowed is obscene. ~~Sa~~ suppressed into ~~a~~ the nucleus of ~~the~~ a frustrated soul

Prince Charles cinema

28 So you thought the fashion brigade didn't bring their Helmut Langs and Margielas to any place that was less than chic and overpriced? When it comes to films – wrong. Hectic international schedules mean that fashionistas are prone to missing films when they're released. This, coupled with odd and erratic working hours, leads them to the Prince Charles and its daily changing roster of films. From Hollywood glam to stylish indies like last year's *Hana Bi*, watch in the company of impoverished students, writers and resting actors.
Prince Charles, Leicester Place, WC2 (0171 437 8181) Leicester Square tube.

Sitting comfortably between Brixton's 'Dogstar' & SE1's 'Last Chance Saloon' The Prince Charles cinema has been awarded 28th place in Time Out's '100 Hippest places in London' chart. As an employee of the cinema I can (quite tinted with bias) vouch for its relative hipness. If only because the staff themselves represent a broad cross-section of this city's young artists, writers, filmmakers & what-not. The environment is certainly one of the most groovy I have ever worked in, largely because my role at the moment is to shovel buckets of popcorn for smiling young things in expensive jackets & then reclining in the back row of the circle, fag in hand, watching the variety of films that Amanda the outrends but heavenly natural projectionist reels out. The Eel, Fear & Loathing in Las Vegas, U-Turn, The Negotiator, The Big Lebowski.
Have some comps for Darling on Tuesday, will invite Farin.

23/2/1999

I dash to my angel at Angel ⊖ where we have a passionate meeting & a brief popcorn fight before heading back to Finnegans Wake, the smiling young Irish barman perhaps entertained by the cabaret mode & swaggering young thingies who are lumped around a corner table squabbling. Perhaps he noticed & recognized Johnny. A cut nose from recent tussles, pale stubble strewn skin, lank black hair over his ears, intense eyes – the Menswear front man looks soon to chart his way out of the post-Britpop swampland that he inhabits. He played me Scott Walker, Lennon & Frank. I'm sure his (the barman's) eyes became adjusted to the sight of Justin Sims. In his parka & brown chords, strangely handsome face, he sat in that pub up to 2 hours before we arrived. Perhaps Justin's horrified face (reminiscent of the expressions that Richard Attenborough gave to the character of Pinkie in his moments of entrapment in the great film Brighton Rock) did draw out of me some pity. Fear as well. A token gesture this, to carry on with this narrative of last nights events, despite the change in my writing tool that has occurred because of my misplacing the pen whilst . . . talking to Justin & Loriki who just came in. More of which later.

A French girl (kelly, em) who speaks not a whisper of English, appeared on the doorstep. Carl met her on his adventures in France. She arrived completely unannounced.

She was at the wake aswell, the poor thing.

Dalston Central is as rough as bleeders. Spent the night at the house that has caused all of this wretched hassle. I, having done my hundred sobs on Sheila's behalf, was less than elated to see her sabotage Justin's 'bond' — the walkman, watch, purse, bracelet & what-nots that he used to secure her the promise of payment. What can one do except express one's disapproval & sigh at the idiocy of the entire sorry show.

Coming back from the wake, Justin heading off into the night, away, away. He tells me today that he slept rough last night.

Lads, Lads, Lads in Reeboks by the telephone box. One in front of me pointing. 'You're sick, You're sick, what are you wearing that hat for?'. Presumably he was referring to my Trilby. I've always thought it rather fetching, and explained to him, quite civilly, that my dad had given it to me. He was not soothed, and spat out worse obscenities than I care to remember. Sheila lost her rag like a goon & I marched on. 5 minutes behind Carlos & Johnny heard the lads muttering bravadoes. 'If he turns around

I'll boot his teeth in?

Back at the flat, Johnny played some most splendid tunes in his role as DJ – Scott Walker, Lennon rarities (including the acoustic rant 'Serve Yourself') & Nick Drake, Faith & Black Crowes to get Steve groovin.

Had a bath with Francesca, candles & danglings on the window. Sex with my most tempting Italian lady has become a daily, nightly, hourly, feature of this wicked film I live. Her full, fabulous breast forever in my hands, face ... out of sight as she takes me full in the mouth with a strangely graceful rhythm. Her eyes with animal lust do shine.

Kellijean, Carlos, Francesca & myself all slept upstairs. Made my way home with a hoover, carrying it around my neck like the arm of a drunk friend.

Seen Buffalo 66, Boogie Nights, Pi (π), Scum, Carry On Spying, Annie Hall, Delicatessen

Theres a song about
a Scouser who went
off to fight in
the Great War,
& saw Liverpool
no more.
I think his
name was
Tommy.

cant get to Anfield
in the 60s, 70s or early 80s, cant
witness the metamorphosis of the poor white.
Archie, you were there ..... shame that your
passion for photography has only recently
let you pick up the camera. Can be here,
there anywhere I choose as the century turns, and
I must let my curiosity reach for the pen,
camera, microphone. I must record all that
excites me & captures my imagination & senses for
a second, where poor white England goes —
how the new England will settle. Black &
Asian are no longer Black & Asian, or anything
else. They must be English & English only.
The term Afro-American or Asian-American is abhorent
to me, and English/British equivalents must
be avoided with a determination unchecked.
Race is not the issue in my work though —
merely love, England & a quest for depth, grace
& charm

A storming reception for my opening set at the Foundry last night (28/2/97), the first time I think, that my poetry has ever been met by cheers & crys of delight.

A great shame that Time Out spelt my name wrong......

—

Met a man from the Welsh Mafia
John Llyod-Roberts, boyo from the Tafia.

—

My financial crisis is now so ridiculously out of control that I have ceased to give the issue any serious consideration. I can only wonder which of my indebted agents will cut the first vein. B.T, My landlady, the taxman, Midland (HBC) Mastercard, the electricity board, the cheque cashing company, my other midland account, Pierre Paulo, Dolly Hill, Phil aaaargh -

£3000 in cash would solve everything with a sensual, painfully pleasant immediacy. Such a sum is only a day dream away, but this reality is unbridged to that paradise where one's imagination is the solution to all anxiety or ill concern. A fairly serious crime would appear to be the only option, lest I enter manhood weary of spirit & perpetually heavy with worry because of these ugly, foolish debts. [illegible]

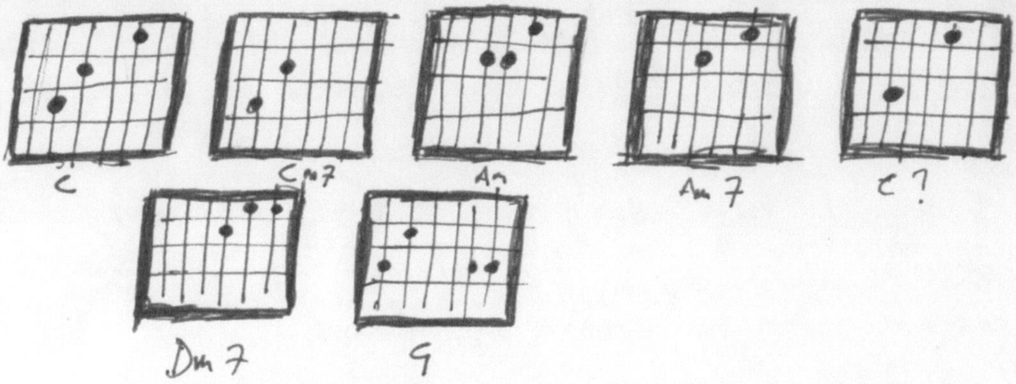

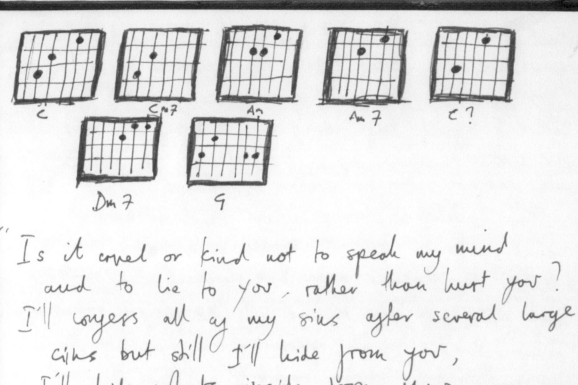

"Is it cruel or kind not to speak my mind
and to lie to you, rather than hurt you?
I'll confess all of my sins after several large
gins but still I'll hide from you,
I'll hide whats inside from you.
I hear alarm bells ring when you say your
heart still sings when you're with me,
oh darling please forgive me ...
I no longer hear the music ....
(…mories of) ~~All~~ the pubs and the clubs and the drugs
and the tubs we shared together, they'll
stay with me forever
But all the highs and the lows and the
to's and fro's they made me dizzy, oh darling
please forgive me, I no longer hear
the music."

Went to a splendid party last week – t'was the opening of a studio in Kentish Town, Blur, Elastica et al on the guest list, Paul Kay (Dennis Pennis) as DJ – Steve, Carlos & myself went along and got rip-roaringly, arse-stonkingly wasted on a fine selection of free Booze and generous passing around of drugs.

Pure, undiluted comedy ensued. Walking around pretending to be Irish or scouse or myself, reciting poetry to Marion's former Bass player (tells fantastic story about his time on tour with Morrissey – apparently Jaime, Marions singer, approached the elusive Mr Morrissey in the corridor backstage. 'Hows it goin' Morrissey,' he asked. 'I'm tired, very tired' came the reply 'But not quite bed-ridden').

Constant drama with Francesca. Rages on the mobile on the way there. Discarded by health – having collapsed, staggered about, vomited, shat [redacted] in the forecourt – somehow ended up in a taxi – speeding through the night bleary to West Hampstead. She must have paid h on arrival. Woke up in one of her tops, warm in bed, where a fight was on the cards, pertaining to my behaviour. Told her I was finishing with her. She wept like a soul in torment. I shed a tear – why? – Because I said that we would spend no more moments of beauty together. The moment was charged with a natural electricity, akin to the bolt toasters with knives jammed in them (mini-cones) swallowed whole, covered with saliva & secretion

Let the story begin ....

My memory is a jar, my sight is blind, my hand has little feeling. The jar is huge, but the hole is tight & rarely can I fit my whole arm in and really rummage. I remember a cupboard under someones stairs, in a small army house. I remember, remembering playing with other kids in or around that cupboard. I remember also remembering falling off of some playground apparatus in a garden somewhere. I remember Amy & a rabbit. Then come the many, many memories of the first visit to Germany. My first home. My father would have been a sargeant maybe, unsure of this. Tall, a sargeant maybe, unsure of this. Tall tall trees – a wonderful garden. A bar in the front room. Feelings of pleasure in the company of girls. The ragged troop of army kids on the estate (remember names like Kyle, John & Ross Hancock): football, kick the can, skipping, bike race's – did I have a bike

My hands are cold on this March midnight railway platform. I will obey the instructions on the previous page when I arrive at Finchley Road & Frog

An excitement was the Ferry. Diving around in a huge pool of balls. Holidays in Italy – driving through Europe. Oh a glorious adventure – going through, under, over mountains.

Kindergarten – someone spilling milk, someone misbehaving. Me perhaps. Seeing my sister go off on her first day at school. Me wanting to join her. Someone telling white lies. Eating breakfast before the light for some reason. Rice crispies.

Waking early & seeing Nan, Vera. Bambinaland & football with the visiting wheelers. An aeroplane. A little motorbike – my dad taking me to the carpark.

Conkers – the smell of army tents canvas. Trucks, uniforms, fences. Feeling my dads muscles. Baths with Amy, swearing 'shit shit, shit' – Amy, even at this v. early age, cunning enough to know how to use this against me. Flying down the stairs. Dad built Amy a dolls house. Fisher price, Soldiers, cars. Games, games, games. Actually flying down the stairs. My little room – looked down onto the street. Krefeld ~~first~~ school – ~~the~~ where we all went – Good Book badges. Egg & spoon race. An old teacher.

chip shop, front of parking space,
Nuneaton 1996? In the battered Vauxhall
cavalier (Blue) – "I can never be happy,
Emotional cripple, damaged, etc".

Sat at kiosk, Prince Charles Cinema.
"What's Fear & Loathing in Las Vegas like?"
"Have you taken LSD?" I ask
"Yes" she answers
"It's that".

9/2/1999

4 .... 3 days to see out before my 20th birthday. I have asked Carlos to cancel my surprise party. He is a concern, I noted before:

'MY FRIEND IS RISING, PACKING HIS GUITAR, LEAVING ME. HE IS AS A GHOST AT THE MOMENT HE WALKS AWAY. DOES HIS SOUL CARRY THIS TORTURE FOR PAST MISDEEDS UNPUNISHED? DOES HE EXIST IN THE SINGULAR? MY FRIEND, A PROUD AND LONELY YOUNG MAN. FIGHTING GODS AND DEMONS. RUNNING ALWAYS FROM DEATH'

This and more, of course. Francesca has given me the surprising, confusing and rather upsetting news that I am to be a father. A mere child myself, in will and conduct, how might I take responsibility for this pill-related fiasco? Something I must do. She sounds sure and frightened & uneasy, & ready to laugh. I must gather my thoughts.

Another concern is my growing attraction to & affection for Lorraine [redacted]: a quite perfect English girl I met briefly as we crossed over jobs at the Vaudeville, and met up with on Sunday for a day of quite unexpected tenderness.

We met as planned outside High St Kensington ⊖

and walked in the cold drizzle towards the park amidst a sorry, soggy crowd of Sunday shoppers & grimacing motorists.
What a pretty picture I paint .... but so light was my spirit as I walked with her. A Ballerina, trained at the Royal School of Ballet, she has grace, poise and an enviable body.
Witty and open - but somehow on guard aswell. Through Kensington Gardens in the suddenly beautiful rain. The green of this city is so sudden, so shocking, I react always as if a mile or three of this sparse open space was Arcadia itself. We sought shelter in the band-stand, but were foiled by a spikey pole fence, and the sight of this unused stage being ~~u~~ equally wet as anywhere else for miles around. On we went, to the Serpentine Gallery, where we with cruelty and interest, gazed at the display / exhibition of various giant photographs. One depicted a scene from some kind of rave or gig - crowd scenes have always fascinated me. The mob — in a Parisian Street or the 70's terraces - holds my imagination in its darkness and mystery. I delight in the sight of unison for any purpose - a gang in the street, soldiers, relay races, uniforms, uniformity: what a challenge to the artistic soul, what a joy for the ancient, animal instinct still screaming

away in our DNA.

We then proceeded to clamber (with some agility I might add) into a locked up boat-shed by the Serpentine. We sat in a boat, smoked a joint. I recited poetry and sang some songs – how twee & tepid that sounds. How innocently comical & sincere: it happened so. Some undetermined space of time continuum went by before we repaired to the surreal cafe on the lake. Cups of tea. Mildly stoned we shared confusion at the food service counter. Brief memories of my v. short spell at the Barbican Centre restaurant come back to me. On went in the rain – and to a church in Mayfair. A more ornate, spectacular & intimate church I never saw in London (the North London Mosque being a different kettle of dogma entirely). We lit candles, and played mock confession in the holy booths. A christening was taking place in the church as we wandered about. We sat briefly. Standing in an aisle I gazed at her gazing at what I can't begin to imagine, her eyes were open, but she looked a picture of pure, holy melancholy. Like a Jane Austen heroine spurned, her profile suggested deeply ~~held~~ felt emotions that were currently being ransacked by despair; sadness, sadness in her beautiful eyes.

Another stop for tea, this time in Old Compton St (we certainly got around, feet & trains by this stage) The rain has turned the air grey and white. A peculiar March mist on around above the busy streets of Soho.

Dukes cafe. Tea. We talked of prostitution, our mutual friends in the theatre (Anastasy proving particularly interesting), Ballet, people passing.

Then she bought me a pint. We meet again tomorrow. I'm off to hers with my guitar.

The housing benefits claims inspector arrives soon. Bastard that he is.

The end of tommorow:

The inspector came this morning: he saw and he approved and he left. Luckily he didn't see meadows scarpering out the back and over the wall. comedy. Then came the horrors, the sordid, the danger of real life. Unexpected the realisation that all is fucked for good. The debts are creeping up my spine. Midland want me in court. Francesca is becoming distant. with my child. Then the worst. My god - must I be deserving of this suffering. Weeping on the Fulham Palace Road almost, suffocated as I was with thoughts of Lorraine. How great is her allure, how mystifying my feelings for her. Another trap set by fate. I catch her eyes and know not what it is I see. All I ever want to know is this: what does she think of me? What does anyone or everyone think of me?

11/12/99

On the Network South East car, the white teardrop patterned window is only to be seen out of with comfort if you have two very round eyes, very far apart from each other, otherwise one can only strain to decipher the occasional flash of light, or stretch up lean down and peer through squinting the eyes mentioned.

I am on way to Germany, hitchhiking and blagging train. At canterbury East the lights as orange kites. I think that is where we are now. I went down the escalator at Camden Town at 15.17. I hope to be in Kregeld for dinner tomorrow. 8pm ish. I don't know how. I couldn't cash my cheque at Victoria, despite getting the company to phone a telephone box wherein I masterfully took on the role of Major Doherty. The Bastard of the situation was that the cheque is perfectly legitimate; only the can't very well contact my father in Kosovo, or my mother in Germany because personal cheques are UK only.

This rocking, whispering, clanging, ringing train is a strange machine. Networks of corridors aplenty. The good British public it serves are reassuringly, predictably, in their place.

The right shades, shapes and sizes. The prose of life in Camden Town at present, eases out of my soul. Instead, the luxurious uncertainty of travel & adventure...

We have stopped somewhere. I stare out of a peephole. A quaint station. Someone is trying to get into the car. I feign sickness in a German accent. Let them go. Adisham: 18:55.

Dover very shortly. Then what. No money or tickets. Unless £15 – can suffice to get me to Calais & a good hitching spot.

Perhaps I can hitch from Dover onto & over on the ferry. I want to get across the channel tonight, whatever it takes.

Strangely, I brought my guitar with me. Perhaps I can busk across. How foolish, naive or impractical am I? How adventurous, capricious or inspired am I? Where am I... Through the peephole on the moving train, all I can see is that the place is quite long in letters and begins with an S.

I think of Lorraine, Carlos, Francesca not at all .... not of anything. I am conscious only of the desire to live.

19:03. Another stop. 'Shepherds Well'. How atmospheric these Kentish stations are by night. The orange light, the cold metal shine, paint old & new. Footsteps. Trees a right shade of green. My attention turns to the alarm chain, for the improper use of which a £50 fine is the penalty. It has been carefully painted red to advertise its most ....

aah, 'Keamsbury' or something not too dissimilar. I believe Dover is but a sentence away.

I remember as a young boy with a big fringe floppy in the little Listurn house. 11 Mountview Drive. I made a fake (17th treasure map and hid it the sloping front garden hoping my sister would find it & be fooled.

I was surprised when my ingenious, calculated plan never quite meticulously pulled off.

7.15. I'm on a P&O courier bus. Going to the Docks. My only outlay remains £1.70 single to Victoria. 65p for a bag of crisps on the train. Ridiculous price.

'Mid channel'

9.00pm? 'Always / never trust a scouser'? Got a free bus (P&O courtesy) to the Docks, where the bright, artificially lit booking hall sits beneath those cliffs. Thieves, gypsies & tramps thronged the outside of the circulating doors. One of whom, a thinning-on-top scouser called Paul dressed in a leather jacket & trainers, overheard me despairing at the SeaFrance £15 foot passenger charge. It didn't quite click at first as he and his roguish companion gestured for me to follow them outside and around the corner. He gave me a packet of Bennies (unopened) and offered me a place on his six-man team. Someone was missing. More of all this later. A French school girl is tapping on the window I sit before. I have waved goodbye to my lovely shore, and will now put my guitar away & report to Paul for my duties in duty-free.

Friday night, Camden Town.

Christ what a couple of days. Arrival in Calais went as well as one might possibly imagine. Despite not having a valid ticket, I was fortunate enough to become quite friendly with the staff at the information desk, even to the extent of singing 'How Love Grows on Trees' over the P.A system. Once on Foreign soil though, things went from grand, buoyant & inspired confidence anew, to recklessness, hopelessness & confrontation.

Lost on an industrial site, but brimming with the new found joy of freedom, I clambered up onto the motorway & trekked to the nearest service station. It was a long way. Still perky enough (after all, I was an Englishman abroad with a guitar and some cigarettes) I began to ask lorry drivers for lifts. The few that spoke English did not have Dusseldorf on their agenda. I simply began to wander, singing & roaring into the starry charcoal sky.

Vive la France.

A cash & carry called East Enders had a food stall in the carpark and at about midnight I arrived there, and chatted to the English lad about my adventures, Marxism & the weather. Cutting him off to approach lorry drivers across t'car park, I was dismayed to see it was the same two that had smirked at my request to get to

Dusseldorf a little earlier. They seemed genuinely concerned for my welfare though, after establishing that I had little or indeed no clue as to how best continue on my way. A lift back to the port where I might fare better for hitching or getting kip was offered. Splendid. 2 more genuinely human ~~English~~ Northern men I never met - and that is saying something.

From Scunny (Scunthorpe) Steve & Paul were Shakespearian in their bawdiness, mocking, comical, caring, innuendo-ridden northern chatter.

Steve bending over to adjust something on side of van: Paul: 'Fookin Ell - ye could park thee fookin bike in that theer Arse. Custom'll probably find fifty fookin' immigrants stuffed up it'.

It was all Johnny Foreigner, fookin' Ell & 'take my advice young Pete.'

I played them a song in the car park and they gave me beer and promises of a lift back should I change my mind about Dusseldorf. I tried hitching for a bit with my sign:

But to no avail. Loads of unreasonable French security chaps & v. dodgy immigrants appearing off of the backs of lorries that clogged the network of concrete parking lots by the thousand. Went for a kip in terminus. Bad more. Every face in there had the look of madness, badness or something far worse than either of those on it. Save of course for the charming & splendid French assistants behind the counter, the place was an island of decrepit species. I silently prayed, inwardly I wept – then I slept. To be woken at about 3 a.m by a ridiculously stereotypical weirdo. Who was I? Where was I from? Where was I going? Did I want him to pay for my ticket? He was a 'very generous man'. My increasingly flustered & attentive dismissals of this wretched specimen, with his sombre English accent & slicked back balding brand of hairs, began to excite him. In the end he was stood before me, looking down at me, making offers that in my small terror I could not quite decipher. A ~~[illegible]~~ French woman saved me, she had been observing from behind the counter and walky-talky in hand she informed him that if he did not get on the ferry now he would not be going anywhere until 5.00 am.

He left. I made my way back to the minefield of immigrants & searchlights to Pauls truck where I kipped. In the morning he dropped me off in Dover, a deserted English coastal town at 7.30 am, and at 9.00 am a standard working class English town with marauding hoardes of young philistines in or out of uniform, plotting their devilish schemes in railway station waiting rooms. No future save for the redeeming sterility of cyberspace and a whole host of forged emotions. They will never know what they should.

Back to London. Sans mobile phone. Damn dash and blast to it all. Phoned mum from Dover and apparently another cheque is coming. Godspeed it will. My debts are rolling up my face.

'Beggars, Gypsies and Thieves'

Back to the scousers at Dover & on the boat. A bigger load of scallies, casuals, tinkers, schemers, warpers, bloggers & dodgies I never took company amongst. They were warm too though.

I sang for them on the boat. Not for the 'lad' lads though, who joked & poked & clanged each other around the head all the while.

One lad, with shaved hair (swedehead) buckled tooth & big feet, was at the centre of the latest anecdote. He had been stopped at customs and deprived of his stash merely because the officer on duty had his suspicion aroused by the fact that someone had written 'CUNT' on his sleeping head with thick lipstick.

They were all 'runners', fetching back duty free by the hundreds. I was offered work an' all.

Francesca is not pregnant after all, although she was terribly ill last night and must wait another 3 days for a final, decisive test.
Everyone has disappeared.

Always on my mind,
my money that I
the money that I don't have
the money I owe, the money I need —
never the money that I have squandered
and spilt on whatever would get my hand into
and out of my pocket as quickly as possible.
Always I think of the money I owe, the money I need,
never do I consider the money wasted.
Equally I brood on the love that I desire, the
love that I long for — never the love that I have
or have had and have cast aside.
Key and knives and candles

Plastic'd

I am studied now in people,
through observation & interaction.
Community police officers and new to the
city provincial flowers tarted, and ~~plasticked~~ up to
lose themselves. If one has the will to
fail there is very little another can do
to encourage a positive attitude. This I
learnt from talking to a fat man in a
Coventry City shirt who stank to high hell
of vinegar.
He taught me other things too, he
would sit me at the bus stop and point
at people laughing & enjoying their
Saturday nights. He would say:
'Are they enjoying themselves?
No, they're destroying themselves.

Tipping his chin ~~towards~~ to his chest, and
quickly flapping his thin, elegant hand
around his ~~[illegible]~~ dark mop of hair; ~~[illegible]~~ Peter
~~He~~ adjusted his hair in the blurred reflection
~~on the top~~ of the small metallic napkin dispenser.

Looking up he ~~was~~ found himself eye
to eye with the fat foreign girl who ~~[illegible]~~
~~[illegible]~~ was serving him. A ~~red splash of~~ blue biro
stain ran down the front of her Kapital
Koffi uniform, and blue ink was in patches
on ~~her [illegible]~~ one of her hands and around
her lips. Lips that smiled a pleasant / friendly
smile – not something Peter felt

partial to at that particular time,

'Anything else?'

'No, just the coffee thankyou'

'Ninety five pence please'

'A pound'

'Thankyou. five pence change?'

'Thankyou'

'Thankyou, bye bye, Hello

there what can I get you...

Peter cursed himself and the universe. The damned blasted waiting universe that he suffered in. Such was the effect that Lorraine not being there at a designated time had on him.

He had circled the fountain 4 time, smoked three cigarettes, read two paragraphs of his ~~the impossible~~ book, and ~~heaved~~ heaved out one enormous sigh of despair & anguish, when a figure bent down at the window of the jewellers along the parade, caught his attention. It was her. Panic.

A quick kiss-cheek or twenty, a practise run of greetings, a giddy walk over.

'Hello'

'Hello'

She was taller than he remembered, and twenty times as beautiful. This thought remained ~~with him~~ only thought for an infinite five minutes, during which time he passed himself off admirably as a small-talk conversationalist with a ~~f~~ cross-fire question & answer sequence on such matters as the weather, ~~late~~ stalled trains and what not.

The walk up the high St in the rain was a nervous affair. What they talked of neither would remember. The park, their destination, would prove to be their stage, the theatre for ~~this~~ their inaugural performance as young companions. Two people alone together in the city, ~~aside~~ who, aside from any chance or spectacular

encounters, have for the space of a
few hours, nothing but each other.
Or, nothing but themselves.

Junike
Camilla
Evelina
Jackie
Sandra
Susan
Francesca
Carline
Belinda

Low on a parks carpet or
high in a tower, the absurdity ~~[illegible]~~ or
my body has endured ~~the [illegible]~~
~~[illegible]~~ of my mind — my
mind has suggested for the
tactics of my body

You can love a girl you will
never see again,
You can love a girl you have
never seen before,
but never can I love a girl
I can't see there and then
and when a sigh continues the
conversation, with no words, only
the distant roars of lovers traffic,

You got a cowboy boot full of weed
Your eyes look like two small green seeds
Your hair is all unk ~~out~~ stringy and grease
Your constant grunts & burps
disturb the peace

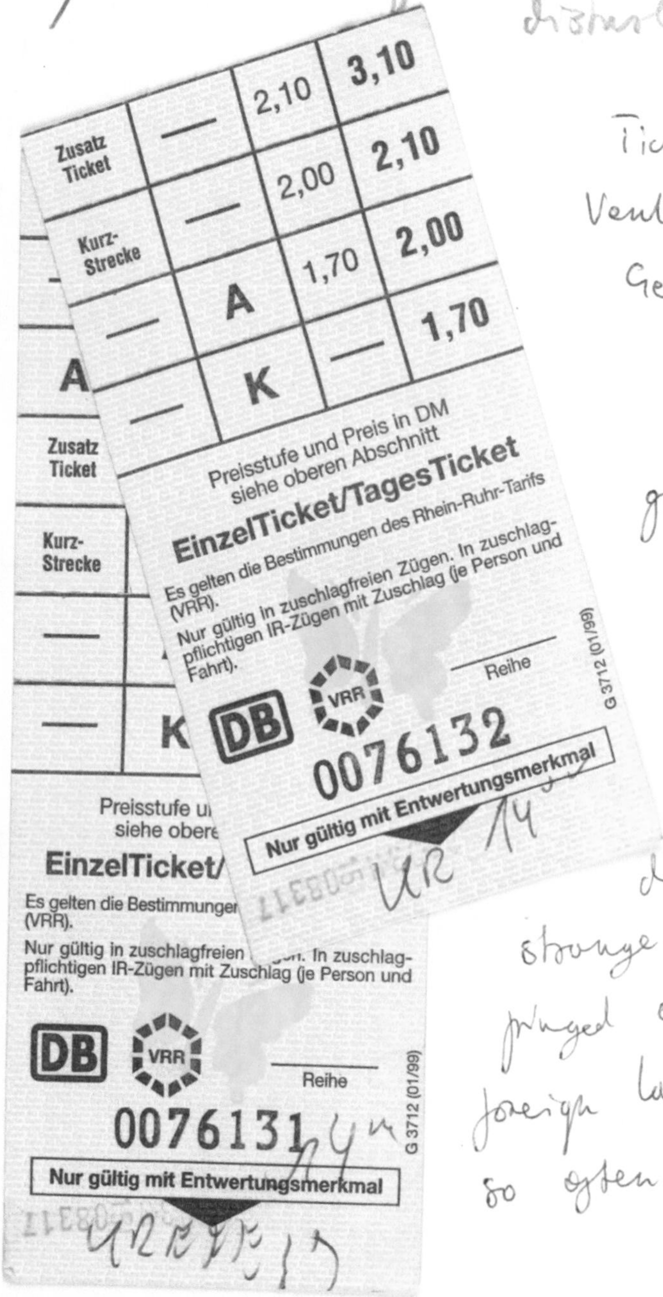

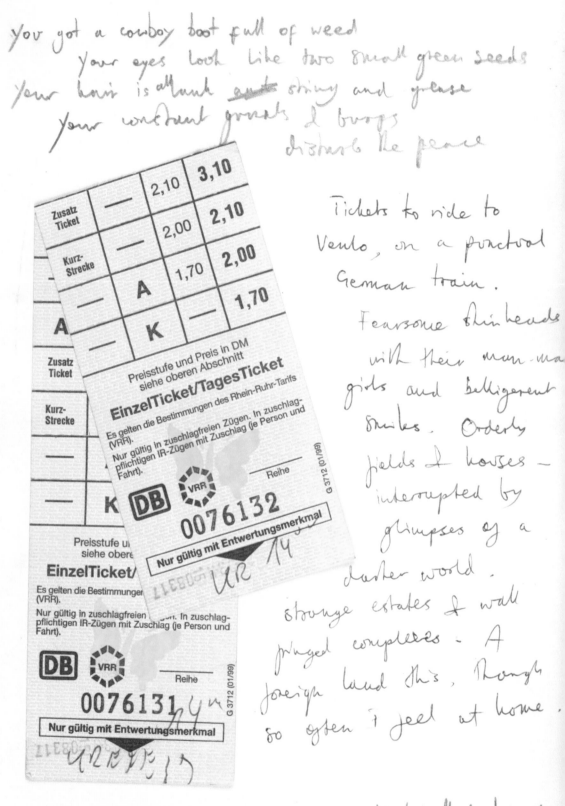

Tickets to ride to Venlo, on a punctual German train. Fearsome skinheads with their man-ma girls and belligerent smiles. Orderly fields & houses — interrupted by glimpses of a darker world. Strange estates & wall pinged complexes. A foreign land this, though so often I feel at home.

An idea — a merry, dishevelled band of tramps & drunkards stumble upon a large sum of money.

Recent books

Lawrence Durrell.
'The Alexandria
Quartet'

Simone de Beauvoir
'The Blood of
Others'

Truman Capote
'Breakfast at
Tiffany's'

Anthony Burgess
'Earthly Powers'

First night of the club tonight
Joshua, Louis, Carlos & I are doing it.
Came home from work & all my records
are gone. Stormed to the Cambridge and
berated the pigman, after a long and bitter
little exchange with his boss. Then I
had a spot at the Poetry Cafe. Went
down a storm. Gigs a plenty at present.
Tomorrow (28th March) I am at the Groucho
club with the Paradigm Poets. Finnegans Wake
(Long Word with Sam Rolls) could also be on the
cards. Work a plenty on the poetry front.
Work a plenty at Prince Charles.

'Old Compton Street, mate, as just
as you can'.
The cafe scene of chocolate &
sandwiches. So many secrets.
Round the corner from Dean St &
the Groucho club, where I performed
alongside Victoria Mosely (The hostess),
John Citizen, Francesca Beard,
Graham Roos, Cynthia Hamilton,
Brinsley Sheridan ~~etc~~ &
a guitarist/singer
Piers Faccini

The design of the catholic church on the Holloway Road — a sixties architects wet dream. High, elongated walls, in turn curled & pillars straight with aesthetic malice.

Friday 23rd April 1999

Peter and John have discussion on linguistics and their relation to the primary emotions. Steve sniffs a marker pen. Sasha sits beneath a blanket. Carlos is being repremanded for lateness. For the best part of this afternoon 'The Libertines' were resident at Daylight Studios Kentish Town — our first rehearsal, and a chance for everyone to finally see what Sasha's drumming is like.

we went through some songs with quite spectacular groove — Pay the Lady, Breck Road Lover, Lust of the Libertines, The truth & the light — and others with a combination of ill-vibes & lack of practise - like You're my Waterloo. The Domestic is coming on.

The studio bloke was smacked up to the eye-balls. Nothing of great import to relate other than that we do seem capable of great things occasionally, and with training and a strong wind behind us, great things will no doubt become daily occurences.

I must make note of all that happens – great insights & mind-altering experiences are no more significant to a diary than everyday tittle tattle. All the better if the tittle tattle itself is of radical proportions.

Some vox-poppy style entries now. Imagine if you will a psychedelic Saturday night in the west end – the dark end of a day that will be held dear, Leanne, Steve and myself headed off to Brick Lane, to Linda. Then a taxi in the rain to Amanda's – that mythical figure who will help us become whatever we become. Then a libertines gathering foiled. Sasha saw Steve and stormed away and off, leaving John, Johnny, Leanne, Carlos, Steve & myself to go and watch Boogie Nights. Most entertaining, especially on sub-standard Acid. Had the whole upper tier to ourselves and acted disgracefully – with bellowing, smilling, smoking and hysterics.

Back to the afternoon – stood on the corner. Hackney Cabriolets in short supply

This flat, a collective of misanthropes

Francesca appeared before me outside
he Prince charles cinema. She raced
to me and kissed Carl.

free e-mail prog

PRINCE
CHARLES
CINEMA:LONDON

26th April 1999

I have been at the Prince Charles for a few months now, and still remain quite charmed by the place. I shall be sorry to find myself sacked, although this now appears to be the likely outcome of recent events. My perpetual lateness has got the shoes squeaking in the corridors of power & the toe within will certainly strike me should I be late just once more.

I seem to recall coming here quite regularly for a couple of years before I worked here. I certainly recall one occasion, 2 years ago, I stumbled in out of the rain with a girl on my arm, and immediately fell in love with the place. I may even have asked about vacancies. I don't remember what films we saw, or who was working, but I do remember

the story being a tad aloof - which I liked
closer to the present - creeping
forward we are to that moment, then -
when it was the present - I filled in
an application form. And another.
Sometime close to the day that Carlos & I
watched 'Love and death on Long Island'
(and afterwards paraded through the tea
rooms of Piccadilly) we both filled in
application forms and were très excited to
be invited to the same group 'interview' -
twas more of an audition though.
I got the post. Carlos never. This did
not bring any animosity - we both know
that success for either of us is magnified
a million times if it is shared by us
both.

But hey ho and never you mind the acute
psychological burdens this most splendid
and dark relationship heaps upon me.
I got the job and was quite rightly
delighted: soon I was swanning about the
place, feeding myself fat on self-popped
corn and watching film after film after film.

Soon it dawned on me what a grand little thing this job is. My ridiculously shambolic financial situation is somewhat eased by the £4.50 per hour I earn & the £20.00 a day that my till scam promises. I know - a complete lack of guilt or conscience is a bad sign for anyone thinking of knocking up a character analysis. So be it. Self-anal is a tricky area. Under this dandyish, frivolous, artistic exterior sits a pensive, ordered fellow - under whom lies an even dandier, camper chap. And so on. Perhaps one day my character will form.

Well, my lateness at the Prince Charles was soon picked up on and I was summoned to a disciplinary hearing and given a warning. I have since been late on more than one occasion and today recieved the letter attached.

Distrait - absentminded or abstracted

!

* Natacha *

The name of a girl I work with. A french girl, a Negress in Nikes. Black, black hair bunched up in dreads over her sweet coffee-coloured face. You could probably squeeze this pencil between the gap in her teeth. She used to dance I believe, now she is training to do something or other — something to do with design. She wears a tshirt over trousers, is very forthright, and lives in W2. She gets worked up quite easily — going red in the face when arguing about starvation in the 3rd world or drugs.

&

Natacha,
if I ask her;
would she
say 'Oui'?

Prince Charles has a similar painting style to Adolf Hitler

!!!Quelle surprise!?!

Just one of those rare & sacred
moments that we all, as men,
can dream about for an eternity.
Mystery, adventure and every
delicate pleasure of the senses.
There was I, drugged & drinking
past the drunk stage, spread-eagle
in the smoky corner of an anonymo
London club/pub/cafe/High St/
church/graveyard etc. The place
remains namele
She comes over, completely
unannounced, and before I
can fully take in the
full meaning of her presence,
her beauty, her grace, her
heaving bosom — she
has jumped astride me and
is grinding away and
tonguing & swallowing my ~~SA~~ Sam
via my oesophagus. She then
hitches up her dress, pulls down
her knickers & fucks me till I
die. She then leaves me with

from 'A Diamond Guitar' by Truman Capote

"Except that they did not combine their bodies or think to do so, though such things were not unknown at the (Prison), they were as lovers. Of the seasons, spring is the most shattering: stalks thrusting through the earth's winter-stiffened crust, young leaves cracking out on old left-to-die branches, the falling asleep wind cruising through all the newborn green. And with Mr Schaeffer it was the same, a breaking up, a flexing of muscles that had hardened.

It was late January. The friends were sitting on the steps of the sheep house, each with a cigarette in his hand. A moon thin and yellow as a piece of lemon rind curved above them, and under its light, threads of ground frost glistened like silver snail trails. Tico Feo had been drawn into himself — silent as a robber waiting in the shadows."

joint & untouched Bloody Mary. Bargain.

Sunday 9th May 1999

How long have I been here? The place has a timeless quality; a mystical, engulfing ~~air of~~ timelessness. Sirens, screams and bells from the outside world are imagined – just as my life, my real life, is merely a dream. The room is blue at night; a solitary navy tinted bulb clipped to my dysfunctional record player sprays the white walls and purple drapes with a celestial fervour. The demons wash away in the ~~light sea~~ sea pinpointed or are 2appear by the laser or burnt by the orange glare of ~~outsides~~ streetlamps outside; A naked negress plays a trumpet, Hancock smiles dejectedly, Lou Reed is ~~smokes~~ blurred under big 70's shades – these are sleeve covers on the wall. My kitsch, kookie decor. The fluffy white rear of some French porn kitten on a postcard, flowers, stills from The Loneliness of the Long distance runner, Quadraphenia, Godless night, Darling. Sinatra under a trilby. Books, books, records, books, a 70's soda spray, a map of central London.

But what is that I see high on the wall – it is the latest addition to my range of poncy, self indulgent stills and snapshots. It is not an anonymous German actress, or a Prague bridge, or a dead comedian, or a lover. It is sasha & monkey, on an A4 faded black & white print. Actually it is not so much black and white as varying deceptive shades of grey. She kneels, naked, monkey preserving the greater degree of her modesty. The camera rests on her slender thigh, blanketed behind by a rushing swathe of light, pointed at the mirror.

Ah – here she comes as I write. Seemingly a little more serene than of lately the loony lost the plot schizo gassed-out-the-flat booner barmy psycho fairy.

Casting off character assassinations and dismissals of Oxford Philosophy dictionary definitions of logical positivism.

Tyrannical is her psychological, conversational and intellectual manner. Unfathomable are her motives – sound is her process of deduction but entirely unsound are her methods of execution. Equally unsound are the conclusions she comes to when mulling over most issues that relate to personal relations with human beings

A key factor of her discontent seems to be the fact that she does not have a penis as well as a cunt. Her earnings would certainly increase.

This most capricious woman, how she ails me!

The advantages of the domestic situation are really quite numerous, indeed, some might site my scenario as being all but a cushy little number. However, the incessant bombardment of unpredictable tirades of wrath may soon break my defences and so I must break away.

'... it is this that I want to restore into life: just the warm flow of common sympathy between man and man, man and woman. Many people hate it, of course. Many men hate it that one should tacitly take them for sexual, physical men instead of mere social and mental personalities. Many women hate it the same. Some, the worst, are in a state of rabid funk. The papers call me 'lurid', and a 'dirty-minded fellow'. One woman, evidently a woman of education and means, wrote to me out of the blue: You, who are a mixture of the missing-link and the chimpanzee. ~~If there is one thing~~ and told me my name stank in mens nostrils, though since she was Mrs Something or other, she might have said womens nostrils – And these people think they are being perfectly well-bred and perfectly 'right'. They are safe inside the convention, which also agrees that we are sexless creatures and social beings merely, cold and bossy and assertive, cowards safe inside a convention.'

DH Lawrence

The Blue Room.

To be alone is now the rarest pleasure.
Lit up like decadence I lie under a
canopy of blue
light. Only the light here is true.
Not the idle sketches of ~~designs~~
~~for~~ suicide and leisure.
-hat I contrive, to give validity
to my validity.

actors,
~~Poets~~ musicians, hookers and dancers,
they all here arrive at the most unlikely hours
losing ~~themselves~~ in the light they
~~are all but a~~ appear to me a
strange sea of beautiful, poisonous
flowers,
my blue light
~~B~~ shall always water them
for I can't take any chances –
~~in eating~~ shining, as I do, to
bring existence
into my existence.

WIZ
OAKLANDS

*the
peepsters
fly
me
to
the
moon
et years are noisy. very noisy. funny that. more funny peculiar than ha ha though.
I'll recall all the unanswered questions. but then, there's always been too many questions.
it streets saw the birth of a new
a of confusion following
on anand tears
blandford and in Brent
bramcote and on the
road the stars are the same.
the whispers and the motions.

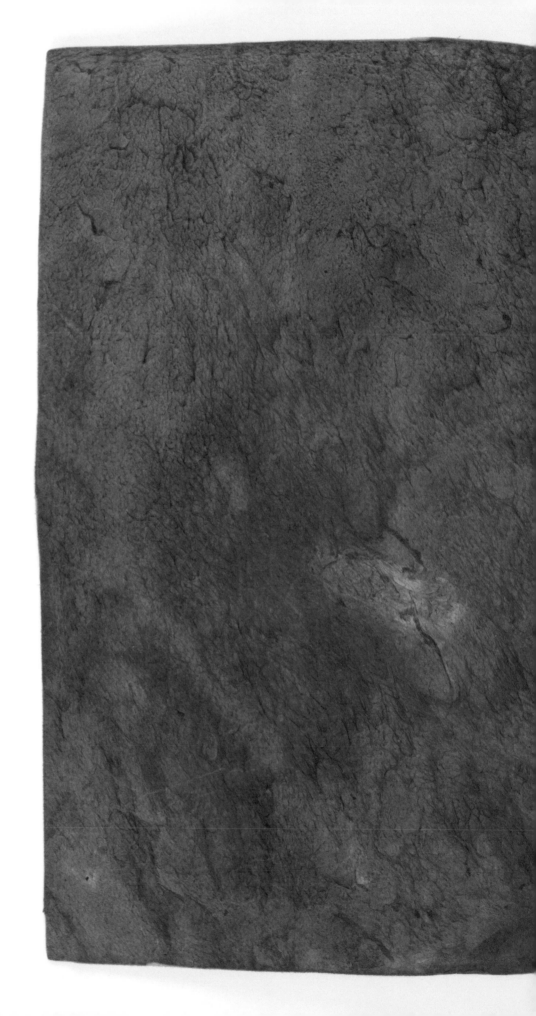

All is altered now. senses frayed, screeching
bones of metal on the tracks. The juice
eaten music from the niggers walkman &
motorized voices. clanging, shrieking
like technology. Melting heels, old
teddy boys, tombstones & oil.
kilo of 70's punk, we're going back
again, to that place we know
no. 15 horse bus. Birds in the serpentine.
smashing up your own town — silent
revolution, you're gonna get what you
want. General strike. Is this
communicating? You must get em out
round here. uniformed Society.
The rod used by the rod. This is wrong,
look at this .... violence breeds violence.
Keep a level of violence, a gas
glow, burn slow — tell the russians,
we surrender & we're not
playing soldiers.
everyone looks the same, we all do, dont
hide. Did you go to the do's? It's
still there. If you can remember it,
it wasn't there. They're all
drugged. Hypocrit — you are,
critic & a hypocrit sucking
on your finger, plastic bags
under your eyes.

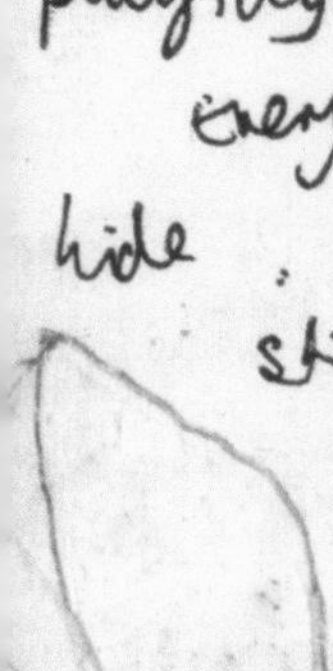

I put the sick pig to bed.
am out strolling ... singing to
myself & walking on me
heels. your love has made
misery distant. to London
quantum ille canis est in
fenestra?
London awake running Alex & I
down picadilly ... avoiding the
whiskey bills. filling up in
the park & strolling past the
policeman in the dark.
Touristic familial endeavours
down on the mall – blowing
the loot in the dive bars
+ strip joints of disney
tacky seedy soho. Emma &
I in the caves candles
dive bar, see the party
people ... on to the social

for champagne & the last
central fugal force of
beagledom. oh Lord, I
come round in this hotel bed,
knowing a cavern. Skin
dry & ugly, how I feel.
suffered enough for vanity
& fame & the despair of
being tuned up to the vast
human caverns of inadequacy
still on the express train,
arranging, fixing matches,
rigging the games, bribing
the ref, oiling the stage.
control? None of it your mothers
a drunk old you're the one
I worship & adore ......
smells like Bankok in London
town oh .... did you get
your fix of flesh today ....

The new Albion rooms careworn
& glamorous as any before.
Already the Arcadian dream
feels the pinch. Rough trade
visitations ... today is that day
that we longed for & what of it?
Piggle sleeps on the cradle-rocking
central line. Pensive, pretty grey
faces changing at Bank. All
week at Nomes are we then is it?
+ a barrell load of songs we're
inclined to be working on. Perhaps
this first day we'll lay down the
foundations ~~to~~,

Skint + minted (split + twisted mix)
~~what~~ a waster
~~Bankok~~
A punch up the bracket
Beggin

Any of that melodious punk,
baby. See Emma smashing
things out of the window already.
She spied bubble related
confessions in my journal and

ent absolutely spasmo.
still she shares my brass bed
+ her soft, sweet
elegance is mine
to adore. Sadness
fills our bones now as
then. I hold her tightly,
get warmth from her. Rest while.
Sense some sanctuary there at the
destination. Smug + satisfied
fella, innocent lamb. or ignorant lamp
B / I / A / E

"Up the bracket"

Saw two shadow men on the vallance road
said they pay me for your address oh I
was so bold .... to say "You see these
2 cold fingers ... these 2 crooked fingers
I show .... a way to mean - no - "

well they didnt like that much I can tell
Said sonshine I wouldnt want be in your
shoes

chased me up three flights of stairs
slapped me in lift + up the bracket
I said oh .... your impossible

Saw the same two men on the cally Rd
Said they doubled that offer I was so
bold , to say " you see these 2
cold fingers , these two crooked fingers
I show ... a way to mean - 'no' "

But it's just like he's in
another world, doesn't see the
danger on show – he'll end
up like Joseph bloody in the
hole, it's just like
she's in another world
so they suit each other
although .... Never get close
it's impossible

well thats no bloody good
Who pays for that?
me, I 'spose

to wander
mouthily!
for all cheers,
is a [illegible]
only [illegible]
the wilder
20 years

Anthem 4 doomed Youth

Bandwagon blues

Are you coming for
a ride
we're going to Arcadia
getting sophisticated at
someone elses expense – our
speciality

Motorhead Strokes
Belle & Sebastian

---

your dog licked my
cuts – is that
right?
is that right?

---

see – you dont know
any different .... you've
always been a cunt it it?

this But rolling heath & country
lanes / the curve of a scratchcard
& the shame of the cold
Some girls are bigger than others
Genius lyricist was the melancholy
colloquial bard of Manchester.
5 Asians staring at me on the
tube, 'its hard enough
when you belong here'

Every line was perfect
up until 1988 come on....
the Rough Trade renaissance
we'll play out this sham, this
hollow sham. I've got so
many names.
Clever boy sick
with love.

the Pierrot Lunaire Club..!
there IS a starman waiting in the sky.
Magick music, live band, performance
high jinx, sweeties, guest djs: Suicide
Wednesday 15th august
Upstairs at the garage
7.30pm until Midnight
£3.00/£4.00 dress to express..
The Liber
Il aura suffi d'un premier
Bracket, voire du seul morce
donne son titre, pour mettre
au top du renouveau rock. Pu
from London, les jeunes gens
niveau médiatique été lancé com
«la réponse anglaise aux Strokes
Doherty, l'un des deux leaders guit
du groupe avec Carl Barat s'exprime
qui nous arrive ? C'est juste une histo
qui consiste à allumer l'ampli, branche
une guitare, envoyer un riff et avoir le
bon look. En parlant de riff, il y a un
m'a flingué. C'est quand j'ai enten
This It, des Strokes. Cela fais
le même. Mais
existé

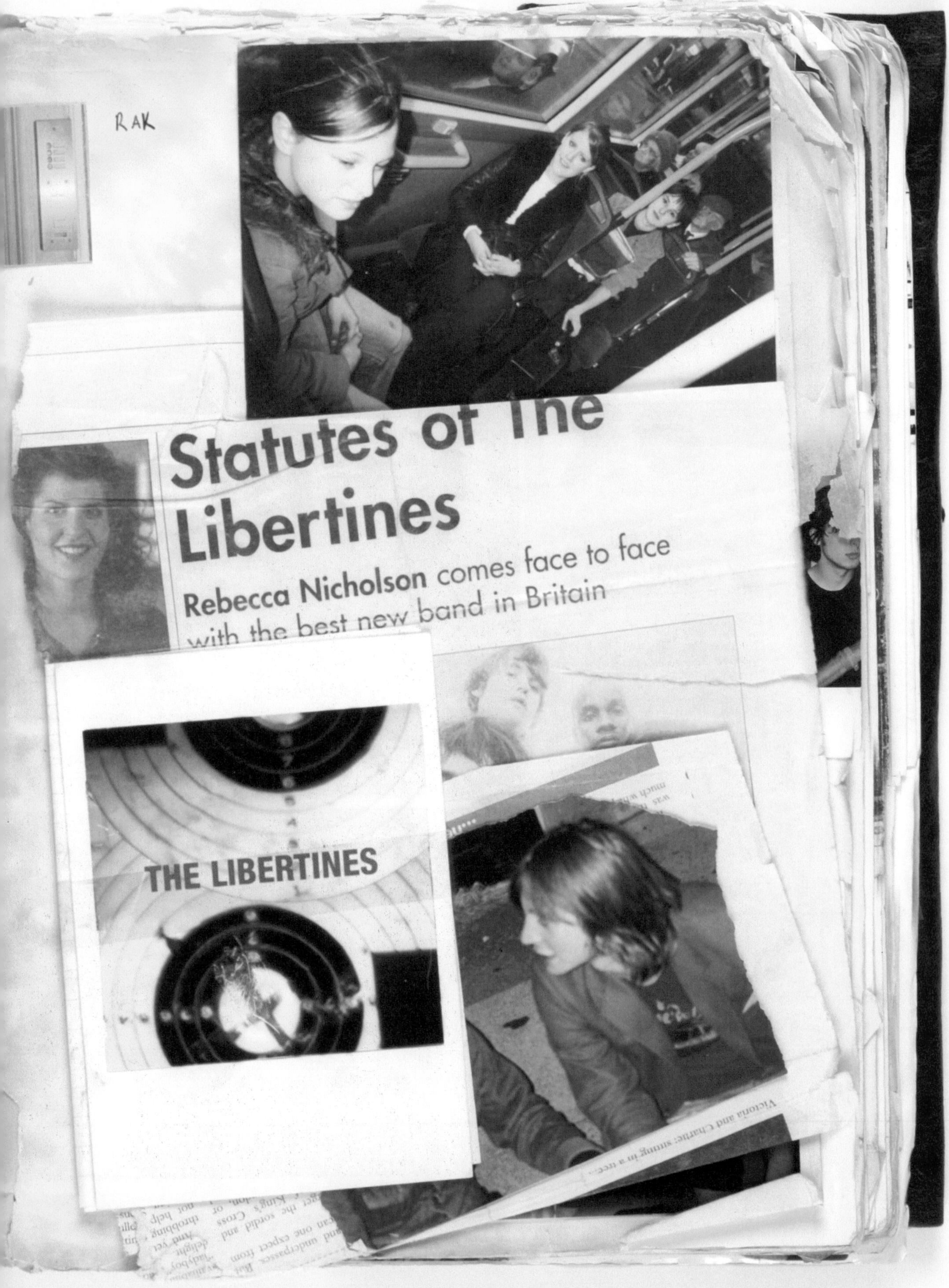
RAK
Statutes of The
Libertines
Rebecca Nicholson comes face to face
with the best new band in Britain
THE LIBERTINES

Th
Liberti
at The Hope & Anchor, 9.30pm, Friday
tubes: Angel / Highbury & Islington

YAMAHA
YAMAHA
RAIN
FAIR
STORMY
FALL
RISE

up the bracket

up the bracke

Me, the Lovely & Chicken
Kirk
x
14/01/03
logh

6.	STUDIO	JOOLS LINK	00.30	[illegible]
7.	STUDIO	THE LIBERTINES 'UP THE BRACKET'	02.40	15.00
8.	STUDIO	JOOLS CHAT TO PETER GABRIEL (INCL VT) + LINK	03.00	18.00
9.	STUDIO	HIL ST. SOUL 'ALL THAT (+ A BAG O' CHIPS)'	04.50	22.50
10.	STUDIO	PETER GABRIEL 'IN YOUR EYES'	04.20	27.10
			00.30	27.40

51.15

52.45

57.55

00A
0A
1A
5A
6A
7A
11A
12A
14A
18A
19A
20A
24A
25A
21A
15A
8A
2A
22A
16A
9A
3A
23A
17A
10A
4A

01TL19CW/062/311001

INNER LONDON AREA THAMES MAGISTRATES COURT

London Borough of Tower Hamlets

Revenue Services, Mulberry Place
5 Clove Cresent, London, E14 2BG
Telephone: 020 7364 4230/4730/4155
Fax: 020 7364 4456
E-Mail: localtax@towerhamlets.gov.uk

Date of Issue 13 JUN 2002

Account No. 1002268083

Summons No. 1141

MR C BARAT
1st & 2nd Floors
112a Teesdale St.
London
E2 6PU

71621006

Address of property concerned if different:

SUMMONS FOR NON-PAYMENT OF COUNCIL TAX

Regulation 34 of the Council Tax (Administration & Enforcement) Regulations 1992.

Complaint has this day been made to me, the undersigned, by a duly authorised officer of the London Borough of Tower Hamlets, that you being a person subject to a Council Tax in respect of the year(s) shown below, have not paid the said sum(s) shown below.
You are therefore, summonsed to appear on TUESDAY the SECOND of JULY 2002 at 2:00p.m. before Thames Magistrates Court at 58 Bow Road, London, E3 4DJ to show cause why you have not paid the said sum(s). If you do not appear, you will be proceeded against as if you had appeared and be dealt with according to the law.

ALL ENQUIRIES MUST BE MADE TO THE COUNCIL TAX OFFICE BEFORE THE COURT HEARING ON TELEPHONE NUMBER 020 7364 4230/4730/4155 NO ARRANGEMENTS WILL BE MADE AT THE COURT

TAX DUE
2002/2003

Previous Years Outstanding	Date Tax Made 6th March 2002	COSTS	TOTAL DUE
£104.55	£725.47	£35.00	£865.02

Dated 13 JUN 2002

Justices Clerk

Account Number	Total Due
1002268083	£865.02

If the amount due plus costs is received by the council before the day of the court hearing, all proceedings will be stopped and further costs avoided.

METHODS OF PAYMENT

Please note:
(A) All cheques and postal orders should be made payable to Tower Hamlets - **NOT the court**.
(B) All payments should be sent to the address below - **NOT the court.**

Tower Hamlets, P.O. Box No. 429
255/279 Cambridge Heath Road, London E2 0HQ.
(open to the public Monday - Friday 9:00a.m. to 4:30pm)

If you require a receipt, please return the whole form and enter 'X' in this box.

If you do not require a receipt, just send the counterfoil only with your payment.

L55E 5360

Live Pictu

The Army and Navy - Chelmsford 12/04/02

Back to Live Pictures

...rty

...return to
...UK at two sell-out
...t London's Royal
...Hall saw over-eager fans
... over the former Smiths
...an's shirts.
...issey himself punched a
... ran onstage during the
... of 'There Is A Light That
...oes Out' on Tuesday
...ber 17) – although it
... to be an accident, as
... invader seemed to
...orrissey's fist.
...broke out in the
...n Morrissey
...shirt during the
...ew it into the
...ses described
...cary" and

Morrissey performed new songs 'The First Of The Gang To Die', 'I Like You', 'Mexico', 'The World Is Full Of Crashing Bores' and 'Irish Blood, English Heart'.

Meanwhile, digital radio station BBC 6Music is planning to record a new studio session with Morrissey to be broadcast in the week beginning October 7.

...y to
...inger

Libertines stir trouble throughout Albion

The Libertines have run into trouble during their massive UK tour, which continues through October.

The band's two frontmen, Pete Doherty and Carl Barat, are known for fighting with each other, but their self-styled Albion Tour has seen the London four-piece get into some hairy situations.

"There's loads of freaks and fanatics at the front – I love that 'cos that's what I am," Pete told *NME*. "We've had a few stand-offs, too. Our support bands have been fighting a lot – **Left Hand** have been getting slowly banned from every venue in the country. The tourbus got bottled in Coventry, although that was actually by my mates. There's always trouble. You don't have to be in a band though, just walk in the streets in a strange town or go in a pub and there's someone who wants to have a go."

The Libertines' double A-side single 'Up The Bracket' and 'The Boys In The Band' is released next Monday.

Libertines fans can hear an exclusive preview of the debut album 'Up The Bracket', release... on October 21, at a series of clu... playbacks. The album playback dates are at: York Ziggy's (October 8), Cardiff Club Ifor Bach (9), Liverpool Krazy House, Northampton Soundhaus, Edinburgh Liquid Rooms and Preston Warehouse (11), Sheffield Leadmill, Wolverhampton Little Civic, Norwich Waterfront, Birmingham Sanctuary, Manchester Star & Garter and Middlesbrough Empire (12), Derby Blue Note (14), Milton Keynes Bar Central and Stoke Sugar Mill (18). Check times with venues.

The Libertine boys in the band are heading your way

BEATLES

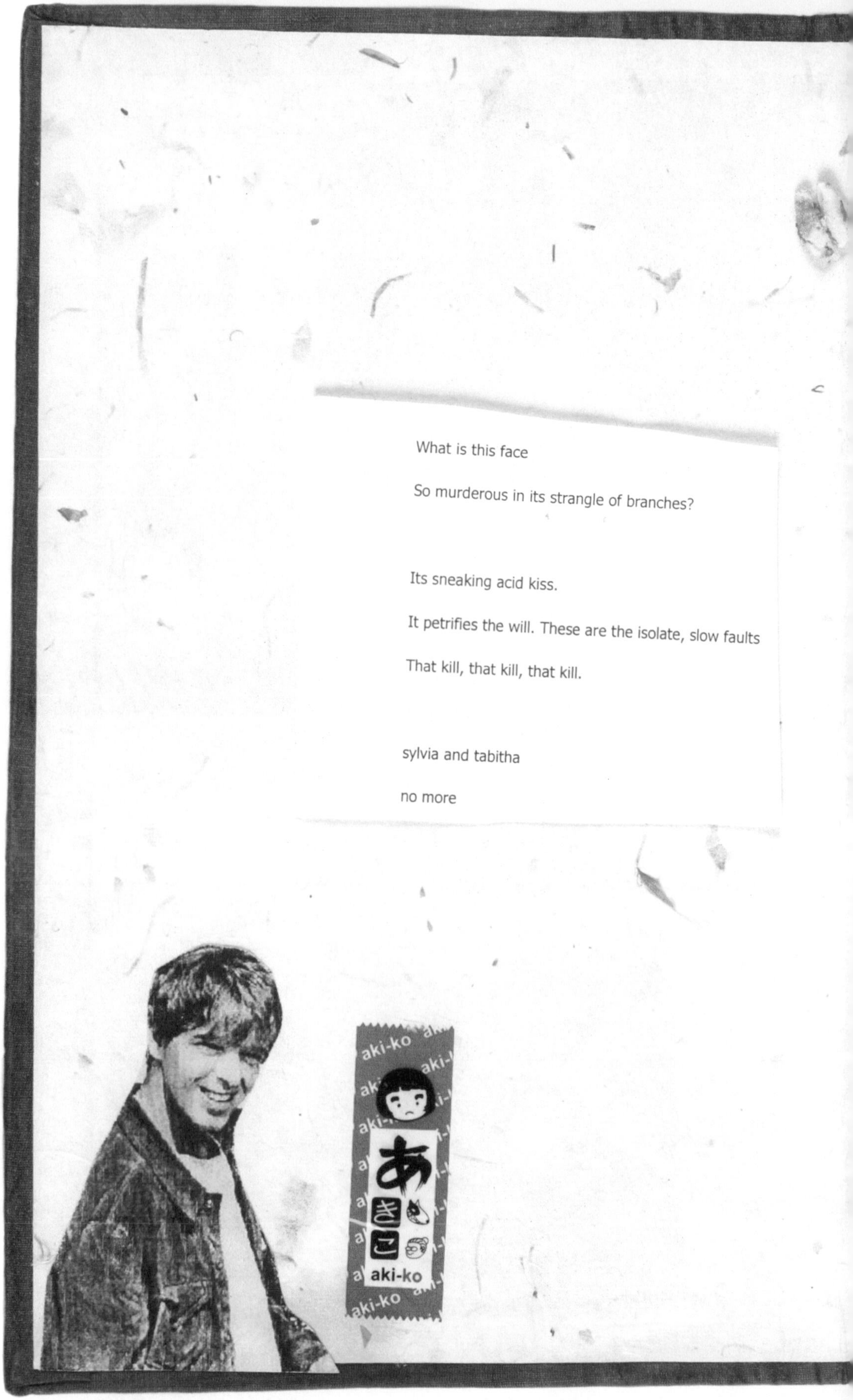
What is this face
So murderous in its strangle of branches?
Its sneaking acid kiss.
It petrifies the will. These are the isolate, slow faults
That kill, that kill, that kill.
sylvia and tabitha
no more
あきこ
aki-ko

The realm may allow one or this month (Albion calendar year) to reclaim
me from the Romans, and present a blank page
to the future naked of date. But we do find
ourself in reflective mood this cold christmas 23rd
day of december, 2002. One ragged roaring hell of a
year wherein The Libertines made good friends & had
some right old knees ups to boot. & they can't
take that away from us. I wonder where Carlos
is this night. Perhaps he has fled to the wilds of
Hampshire to be with his family. So long Marianne,
it's time that we began... the Albion rooms has spent
the last three weeks being shag & boxed up to the
nines, and what tales I might tell. My one
remorse is a heartbroken Tabitha, who I may make
it up with yet, depending on temperament &
weather & alignment of stars.

---

from anonymous: 'SO SAD ABOUT JOE'

Not
Old enough to bleed. what every trick wanted
what are we gonna do now? Taking off his turban
they said is this man a 'jew'? Man I'm
broken want to obliterate myself this christmas
Fuck yeah & get back to London as
quickly as possible. To creative warped
individuals who love me only for an idea
'Tonight, tonight, toni-ght'
And then the gaslight tapes, sounds a bit
like Elvis, a little more morbid; singing Dylan

It's these restless nights I shake up the ugliness
exterior and resign myself to it. If I feel
I could die... then I would die. But d
happier here, mystified if not all sullen
If love is a shadow it crept up on me
there why else mention the thing? No poe
am I now, lost for mystery & romance
pale in the short air, cracked window of a
military bombardments on the scenery. My
peasants heart resents the earth, my Makers
fingers jutter than amateur perfection. Ling
all one cavern, softened to the mossy fur
of smoke that warms me & rolls me aw
like under stones. I coil as for further
shores & resist sleep so as not to resist
the entire day here. Cordial to the low
murmur, I collapse, scratching, light in
collarless cotton

I hope daylight comes soon that I might
see it. It may mark my features permanently
though I fear it is too late already.
"Someday you're going to need me, and I'll be
waiting" I want to keep on living even in
this hard heartened witching hour, "so please
hurry darling dont make me wait too long"

...nds against a wire mesh fence I watch
...usic. Everybody's happy to find we're all
...e same, but we ain't the same if this ain't
gravy train – it's a one way ticket to
oblivion: "Is everyone all right?
coz I saw some kids outside
if they're friends should tell
they don't look well
don't wanna start a fight
(see)
but there's a man on that side
he'll snatch your money
while your busy dreaming

25th 10.00pm awake from libertine dreams crowded/uncrowded ...ena, indoors somewhere, bedroom full of intrigue. Maerent ...ently we're going out for some reason, I hate it. ... knocking about. Photos of Dounes pushing someone ... a retreat atop a windy hill, stacks of records & quality ties, what could it all mean?

"I don't create new things; I bring existing things together. The only element I use is catastrophe. Plagiarism is what the world is about. If you don't start seeing things and stealing because you were inspired by them, you'd be stupid" (Malcolm McLaren)

'I've already tried, she's not interested' The vicious whi
kids by the underpass can't get to my nana's'

['This Perfect Day' The Saints]

see mum's quotat ... prior
may

also opening to 'So it goes' Nick Lowe

clapper board intro 'do us all a favour' that's
ant music rattling worrying me into the night. Go
I keep having flashbacks to the Albion rooms f
seeing the wolfman on his back on the floor
upstairs Nadine on the bed horrified or delighted
I'm not sure, pete with a huge wolf-boner and
his trousers hitched down. He looked at me like a
child and I watched agape as the wolf bone
withered under slacks into a long thin sausage.

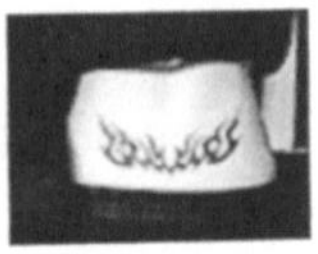
my tattoo

february...

october 2002

may 2002

june 2002

This is 'Hayley Guerrier'
who describes herself as
'pulchritudinous + resplendent'
once more .... 'with feeling'

Scraps of identity, a warped & oppressive system that was sidestepped, and I spiralled untangled embracing nothing out & new sensations, fears & opportunities for the rampant imagination. Alone again or in a crowd, in the heart of London or in a bed in Bilbao. Scaling creaking wobbly old metal pipes up the side of the 'Empress of Russia' pub (now a fish restaurant) a massive old empty building near Sadler Wells that we squatted awhile & had created up nights in, ever a g'ig of sorts .... flying goggles & cranky guitars.

The new rag, lumped in a bin liner with an octopuss' armful of placky bags trekked around Kentish Town, Camden Market, Cobble, Spitalfields & Whitechapels, to the toothless professor of smack Dr. Paul with the campest cameraman & in the rain. Then a meet with Bounds Green's African prince outside Whitechapel tube, rugged loolies at I in military attire & to a ruptured Albion rooms tidied in hours and now lids drawn heated on the eyes. A young looking fella has a crush on me.

10.00-21.00 uur (koopavond).
zoiets vier je niet
aan 'De macht van
Raster 100 dus. Gewijd
het getal'.
nummers van Raster
dezelfde reeks waren Kunst als kritiek
Het mes in het beeld, de eerste een door
Vogelaar bijeengebr
it's not country singers that
most attention.
the new year.

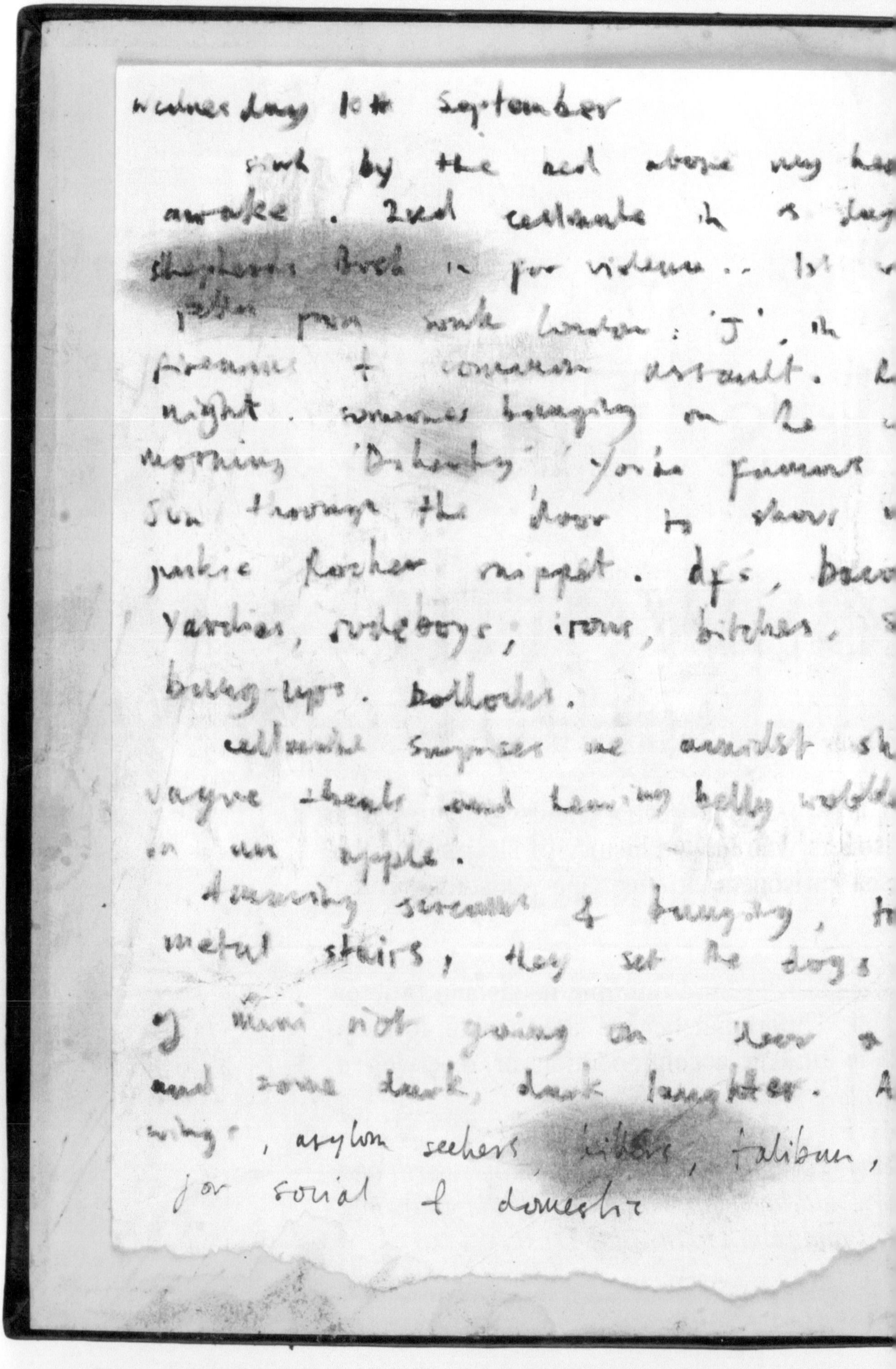

wednesday 10th September

sunk by the acid above my hea

awake . 2nd cellmate is a slug

shepherds Bush in for violence .. 1st

peter pan south london : 'J' . in

firearms + common assault .

night . someone banging on the

morning 'Dickerty' you're famous

sun through the door to shows

junkie Fletcher snippet . dfs , bacon

yardies , rudeboys ; irons , bitches .

bang-ups . bollocks .

cellmate surprises me amidst sh

vague threats and heaving belly wobbl

on an apple .

Amusing screams & banging ,

metal stairs , they set the dogs

of mini not going on . door

and some dark , dark laughter . A

wings , asylum seekers , lifers , taliban ,

for social & domestic

326

splashes me
it your old room
massive flash

possession of
blessing all
door that
! passing the
the, 'jai! jai
swinging lines
s, 23 hr

out of window
sticks of incense

crashing down
'em. Some hits

ly swans screaming
jobs. wings wings

the of clanking

day one in the Arenderan retreat, I awoke congested & wheezed on the sprawling soft leather of the couch where Alan, Carl, Goatee & I my last awake self watched headhunters awhile, I slept....
Wales greets me, we are in the hem of the Brecon Beacons' skirt

Day 2 I come into myself for the very first time, not liking my appearance but aware of evolution & forever changes. Loathe to write & live even cheaper

Some friday and the black hills surround us. Carl has gone under the knife today, after smashing his own face in on the glass sink shelf, after a harsh night of drinking, smoking and rowing....

"ere what about us?"

take an easy graceful sideways position

Resonance fm : 104.4 fm

clambering over wonky miles of time
heading the tumble in rhyme
a jumbled jungle of ill thought 2606
endeavours we'll crack the jackpot
riddle together gazing out of goaties
window, one eyed willie besides
on this rolling vessel into Arcady &
all tumult & woe to overcome
woe the registration, overtaken on
the long grey stretch before us.
Autumn barricading itself in subtlety in
colours mixed and matched,
steady days like a yawn, the nights
silent stillborn cry for the very dawn.
Bales of hay strapped up on the M4
broken boxes on the roadside, weathered
by the years cars crossing lanes like
rubs. Biggles stirs in his sleep
coughing.

Again; a time for
valour. A time of
whispered events. Now jaded
with the passing years.

Extraordinary general meeting 19th Dec 2003

Alan Magee & his partner at
creation (stephen king) tidying up the past &
laying things up for the future. Later Evan
we sit around a table at with
sugary tea, ashtrays,
a degree of that rare thing (harmony)
and glasses of water.
Recording January & Feb,
dates in March in UK, maybe
Japan ... America ... there are a
few immigration issues apparently.
Bilo's criminal past raising Uncle
Sam's eyebrows & stalling the
Albions 'new world' progress.
After the meeting we stroll
down Baker Street to the Sherlock
Holmes hotel, for champagne
& leather seats beside the fire.

christmas 2003 comes and goes

in sweeping light & byzantian

argument. Think back to the 23rd

– the christmas do at the

rhythm factory, and at the

end of the 3-man show in hat

means conducting the crackers

around in some tangled ritual,

spinning them on to further

nights of panic, confusion,
adoration & drunken arcadian encounters
about the decent & cut glass joy
of life that shivered through
the club, the winter
whitechapel club in the city of
Libertines we stoked the fire
once more & paved our way
for handshakes, nose-ups,
signatures, snogs, asides, sweat
squalor & salvation John-less
we braved the set rattly garage
punk attacking the midnite ~~[illegible]~~
with rhyme & treason plotted
thick like our coughed up
bloody jacket bleeding lungs
against the ruling tyrannical
past, the open tasteless former
selves recently exposed so smiley
& clear headed in the
murky christmas night.

chet to ride playing & oh Lord
what a scene earpopping near to
death reckless night I'm lost in
some real place derailed the train
of taunt affection – me in bed with
me affected plaster covering ... a
huge wound? a spot! Sabina Sabina
is telling of her writings & adventures
with hard fellas. More from her
some pages away – – –

Silent nihilist with dyed credentials
curled up still on the
blanket swakened doughnut.
we watch to dribble problematic
lesson) a corner of a film
The destruction of our planets
of my plans, plans for
all to see I float high as
reaching out for all the
stars of the stage have ever
been and salvation – comes
by way of a post . . . .

wait for what?
"I dont know'
Still death haunts the life out of
many a young 'un. I'm staring up
useless now in the inner circle
of my own conspiracy. Heroin
& crack bind my ankles &
scrunts my back ~~of~~ my mattress
my magic carpet whisking me into
Arcady, that warm enchanted
soft forbidden loss I'll be
punished for all eternity all
for ½ ~~and~~ an hour of exception
liberty, lazing along side
the arcadian wench that never
forsook me not for all the
impatience in hell nor all
the dreamy ~~[illegible]~~ darker deeds
that the well-meaning wideboy
wasted love ~~sweetest~~ rarest hours with
Abandon? It rails me, steadve

'Do the most perfect deed you can'

A statesman of all people had said that books of metaphysics can contain nothing but sophistry & illusion'.

Traité des Systèmes.

Thirty steps

I went down with the stairway which sunk abysmally into the darkness below.

A chaos of sordid galleries echoes of horrible silence whose curse I did not discover.

The past & the future are contaminated with doubt & nostalgia. The insuperable oblivion was voluntary, & my escape so unpleasant that I swore to forget it ... and a pattern emerges, a cycle ...

8: / The Lust of the Libertines

F / Bb

The Lust of the Libertines
is really quite tame
it rages quiet nigh here beside you
and your lust for fame
but fame such a sinister game
oh I know ... it could all end this
way then
some things won't be the same
just a face & a name
on a page

but I'll be soundly sleeping, I'll sleep
right through that age
coz I can deal with all the
blood on my shoes & the holes in
my soul

my spirit is tainted all my
tears are painted Am
just so long as you ....
C
dont forget to ...

F / Dm / Bb / C / C7

cut me on the wall
by the graffiti of all the things
I just couldn't say
shove me up the wall
oh my darling (or Poor Cow)
it was a kind of loving but
you left me in the family way
again

F / Bb

The dust on my tambourine
really can be explained
I need to shake it more often
need to shake away the blame
forget-me-nots bloom on this day
then
but they whither with age
the taste of goulash in your mouth
as you stumble offstage ...

Infinite delirious mornings akin to friendship of revelation. Hannah, Sabina & I in bed. I am in fluttering agonies with a gummy eye, vision gutted by conjunctive jelly souping up my sight. The weekend is half full, half empty and as is standard we run the gauntlet of emotions this era fast. For now I can claim comfort and I smile even at Sabina's tales of gangsters and booze and birds of her amazing life, this rowdy decadent darling friend or headfucker, like Hannah she turns life into a film worth watching, drowning dreary days in waters of divinity and surrealist dot to dot that follows the pencil through the dots and forms a silhouette of adventure & poetry and ... why not ... love

the bleedin a
stinking
time
d

Sometimes you need
a bit of stimulation,
the human soul ...
we are de-humanized, spoon-
fed what can be almost
intolerably awful music, film or
whatever medium a once proudly
toted 'art' comes in. Ever heard
'For Lovers' on the MacDonalds
'piped' through music. Highbury
Corner MacDonald it was. Fingy
fingers – strings – sing
Patting the bedsheet, lightly
almost strumming the rhythm on
a thigh clad in denim, with
a sigh, sad in the diamond mine
of the rough soul, dark with
glistens of infinite beauty &
worth, deep in the imaginary
earth.

"I was thinking of you..." he says
"I always think of you..."
we chatter awhile on matters
trivial and terrifyingly
important alike...
He wanders in and out
from room to room. A
walk in his rooftop cave,
elongated lair, wild hair
and unfathomable eyes.
I am begging him for
words... longing for the
exultation A infinite glorious
morning that comes like a
shadow hot on the heels
of a new... Song
Supposed Christian, smacks you
in the gob to put a finely pointed
and the anointed ...

hyper-active drastic brains hopping
about the place, revolting curling
face he

says
"How can they seriously put a man
in the dock, who has just
been to Thailand with
Dot Cotton, on a charge of
possession of a dangerous weapon"
other motto's of the profession
(I say often without knowing which I
am conscious of but anyway....)
a very dull & psychotic all at
once little

hand over the mouth tha

Just understood why some rude

boys tuck the trousers bottoms

into their socks

jump in every
doors
in the cellar
sooner
in the Myrdle
St
on the beat
workin' 'em
over

police
as English
as a

or a

(both made in Formosa)

Cant stand me now [Doherty/Hammerton]

Last Post [Doherty/Barat]

Don't be shy [Doherty/Barat]

The man who would be king [Doherty]

Music when the lights go out [Doherty/Barat]

Narcissist [Barat]

The Ha Ha wall [Doherty/Barat]

Arbeit Macht Frei [Doherty]

Campaign of Hate [Doherty]

What Katie Did [Doherty]

Tomblands [Doherty]

The Saga [Doherty/Roundhill]

Road to Ruin [Doherty]

What became of the Likely Lads [Doherty/Barat]

they meant it ~~and~~ so so it was meant
to be ... they've all got it in
for me

so someone'll have to pay
someone'll have to... greed

save me from what I want
" ____________ " need.

saw the fuse
it's gone
it's gone and ~~won't~~ ~~be~~ ~~given~~ ~~happen~~ back coming back
~~he~~ gone and won't be
undone
the whole shebang, a plan
planned it out on a towel
all the guys are going back
oh I aye
plan A not going for intimacy

ripple

and I know what it meant to be
all got it in for me
oh they call 'em the Libertines oh they
ain't Libertines

I thought that you had a clue
can't you see what they're
doing to me?
and they're getting away with it
coz you're standing back &
taking that shit
believe it's love...
if it happened to you
what d'ya think you'd do?
you and I done it all
understanding when you're standing
against the wall
but I wouldn't do that to you....
now guess what I'm going to do
when I catch up with you
put into action
what I've been feeling
you're so -- any idea
no don't come near
I've no idea what a person can take
all these thoughts & I get nasty too
yes I will my boy
search & destroy

PAGE 14
SUNDAY MIRROR, July 4, 2004
VOICE OF THE SUNDAY Mirror
voice@sundaymirror.co.uk
Cost of sex, drugs and rock 'n' roll
ROCK music is littered with the bodies of those who let the good times roll.
Sex, drugs and rock and roll... too many stars have tried them all. From Jim Morrison and Jimi Hendrix, to Janis Joplin and Kurt Cobain. Great talents destined for an early grave by drugs.
For decades they have assumed a treacherous glamour, made more dazzling by the knowledge that the greatest rock stars, The Beatles, Rolling Stones, the Beach Boys and all over-indulged.
heroin and crack cocaine.
There is nothing cool about a
could have had it all and finished up

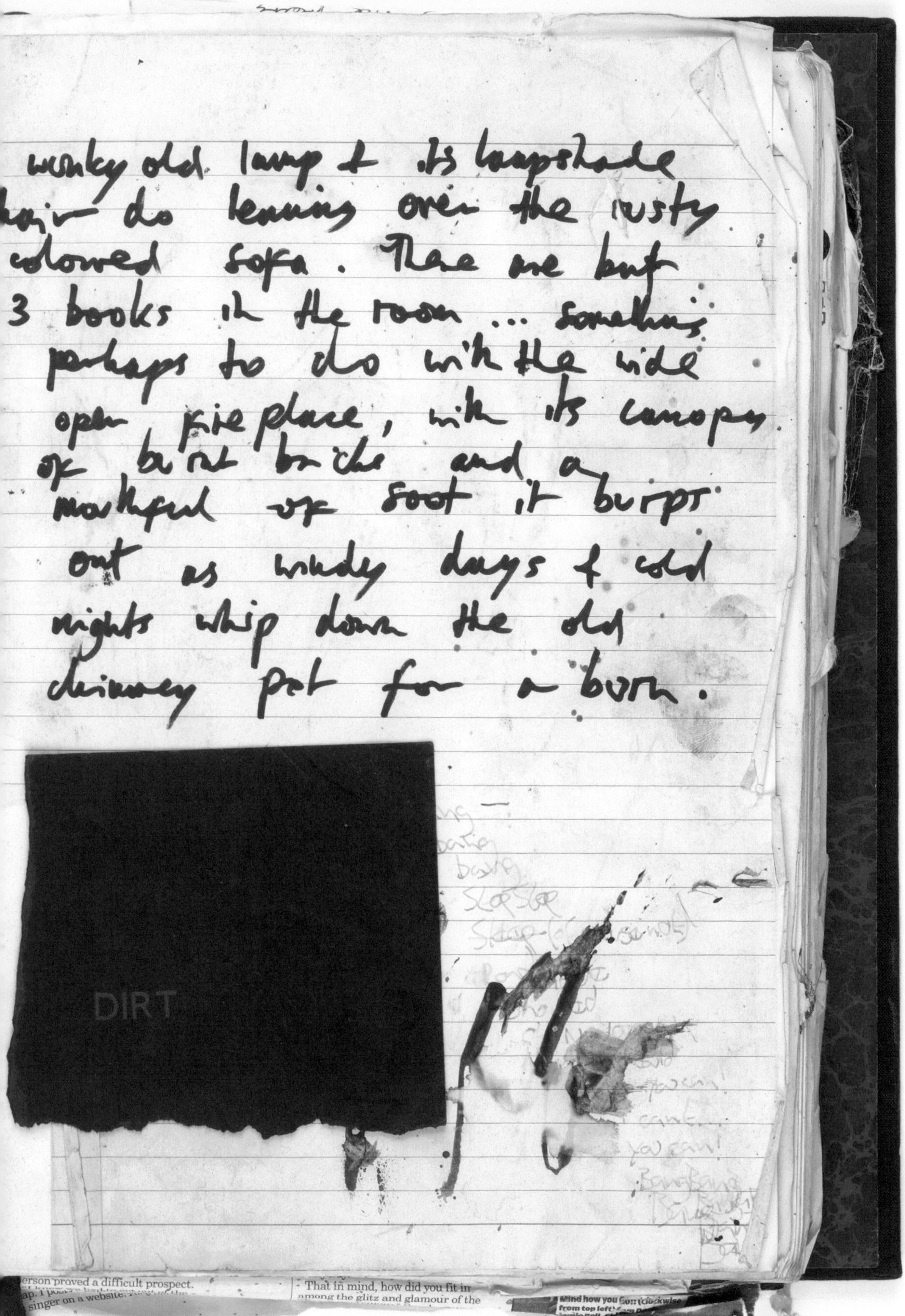
wonky old lamp & its lampshade
hair-do leaning over the rusty
coloured sofa. There are but
3 books in the room ... something
perhaps to do with the wide
open fireplace, with its canopy
of burnt bricks and a
mouthful of soot it burps
out as windy days & cold
nights whip down the old
chimney pot for a burn.

DIRT

erson proved a difficult prospect.
singer on a website.
- That in mind, how did you fit in
among the glitz and glamour of the

Shamble do we through & across Kingly
cross streets & alleys streaked with
gloomy yellow lamplights & hypnotic red
bulbs spelling 'vacancies'. My vacant
smile is neck & neck with a ~~genuine~~ gaunt
& grinding sullen teeth sinking sadness,
on a collapsed bed Clara holds a wine glass
& measures up to her shadow or the duvet.
Drew strums one old Gibble and melancholy stains
slip out from under rolling caressed chords of
~~co~~ ah but what use is a melodious soundtrack
to this surreal & touchingly tacky scene

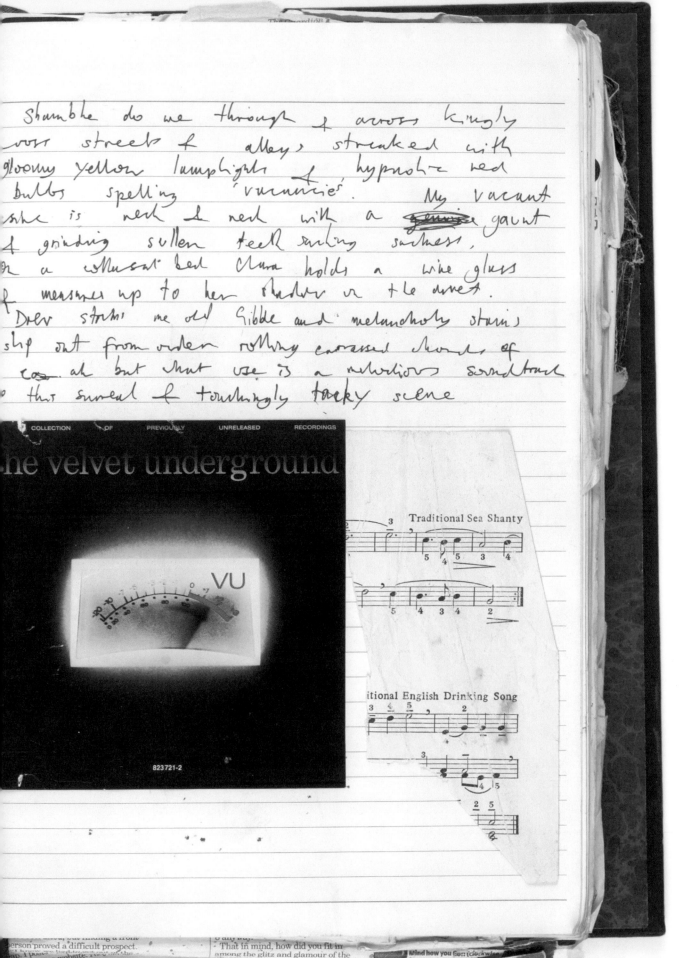

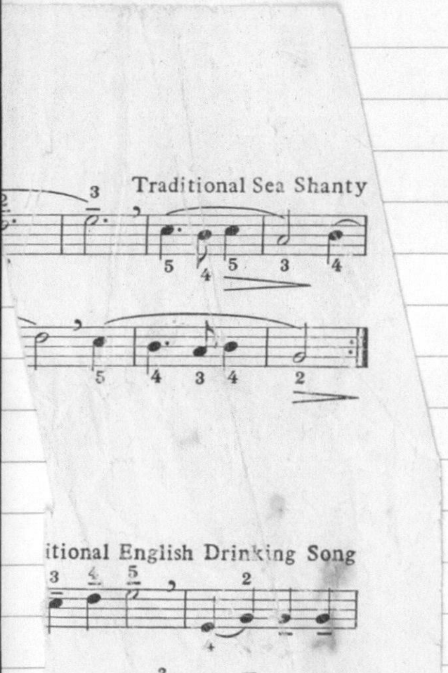

person proved a difficult prospect.
singer on a website.
That in mind, how did you fit in among the glitz and glamour of the
Mind how you

drinking whisky in a brave new afternoon,

jostling for position in Peter's ~~popularity of~~ ~~pos~~ presence, everywhere ... I'm walking like a cyclone, indeed a magnet for yeah yeah yeah rar rar pepped up and paranoid and pranged at the merest imperfection am I as ever ... but still I can't be permanently deluded please ?! Something is afoot tonight tell ye ...

wrapped up in blankets and melodies, Sara speaks softly and with a cigarette flavoured hush) tattooed & halfway to hypnotizing this wide eyed boy from free-cloud 9. The polizei came round last night, and not to present me with an end of term bouquet. People filled up my room after the gig and hotel staff went into panic mode.

The Guardian

how do things become so and so complicated ....?
these simple matters of inconvenience, mishaps
and misunderstanding. I said i'd play
Daisy's birthday party and Daisy's birthday
party I shall play but Char has kept me
beating heart jumping and blood a-pumping
through my paranoid brain with his
most drunk (?) dishevelled shambles
of a shoddy & very very sad set events of.
Taking my long-prized fog down hit not
to me but to the Pleasure Club ...where
the party is is. uh? James allowed him
to take my precious tings tonight - another
epic managerial fuck-up. why can no one
do the simple things with any, even
a smattering — of efficiency.
Listen to me! the shoddiness
of em all ... but I
mean really. if anything has
been clear this time past its that
I want my stuff here
Char mustn't be given responsibility, ...

more or less do you know the
question again and rookeries a
murder of crows. it's his downfall,
long sullen too smudged to be
sinister stares. watch it happen,
watch the cockled egg cuckold
collapse, sombre soaking we hunch
down slurp and squirt your poison in
the eyes of the wide eyed wonder
kids 'come and see the blinding'

blinding the blinding

person proved a difficult prospect.
a singer on a website

- That in mind, how did you fit in
among the glitz and glamour of the

Mind how you go: (clockwise
from top left)

The Guardian the good old days
new ... [illegible handwriting]

...mes his muse

teacher wails, "I just need a little bit of time to plan"), and the interval slightly dissipates things, but this remains an impressive production of a promising new writer's work.
Elisabeth Mahoney
Until October 23. Box office: 020-7610 4224

Pop

Babyshambles

Scala, London
★★★☆☆

When Pete Doherty first started moonlighting from the Libertines with Babyshambles the result was just that: an inept, childish scrawl of what a band might be. It seemed obvious that without Carl Barat as foil and spur, Doherty's muse could only wreak a hollow kind of havoc.

All of which makes tonight some kind of miracle. Doherty is a star — here's a novelty — by virtue of innate charisma, a force of feral intensity and hypnotic otherness. It's a force, you sense, that he can't always control, it batters him this way and that but, for now, it's as if he's realised he must stop messing about. The new look Babyshambles are muscular and tight in a way the Libertines — a tense, nervy and notoriously unreliable live band — have yet to master. There are marvellous new songs, too.

Unsurprisingly, much of what was great about the Libertines is here too: the ferocious energy, the elegant lyricism, the way the band recall the Smiths without ever sounding like wan Smith copyists. In Fuck Forever they have crafted a future anthem, a peculiarly English echo of Smells Like Teen Spirit that is monumental.

What a pity, then, that a third of the show is ruined by the appearance of inveterate scenester Dot Allison, who may or may not be Doherty's new girlfriend, fresh from droning through the Liz Fraser parts on tour with a somewhat hobbled Massive Attack. (She has already been dubbed Yoko Ono; in truth she has a fraction of Ono's talent.) Let loose on songs both old and new, she sings like a tone-deaf schoolgirl and plays the glockenspiel with all soullessness that can be telegraphed through a stick and a strip of metal.

Still, someone living as hard as Doherty will make as many bad choices as good — as anyone who's hitched ...

Last night's TV

Who's a clever boy, then?

QI (BBC2) is back, with Stephen Fry looking like a professor of Ancient Greek, who, through some frightful government initiative, finds himself in charge of Bash Street's sin bin. Not one of whom has done his homework and most of whom have no homes. Naturally avuncular, Fry comports himself with benevolence, ejaculating rarely heard ejaculations like "Oh, lordy, bless!" Who can fail to pity the man when he incautiously mentions that, when a rosy-kneed schoolboy, his tailor was called Gorringe. (This was apropos a rhyme for orange, the only other suggestion being Lester Piggott asking for porridge). Bash Street licked its thin lips. "Which side does young sir dress on?" they whined lasciviously. "Would young sir like to wear a cravat on the cross-country run?" "You are all such beasts" cried the tormented man, thrashing like a well-educated whale.

(Fry Minor can count himself lucky. My school uniform was a djibbah, a sort of Arabian sack, it being the view of the maiden ladies who founded the school that growing gels have no shape or, if they do, it is far better covered up.)

QI, for Quite Interesting, sets out to show that we know nothing much and what we do know is Quite Wrong. The Bash Street gang are media wits to a man but they are null and void on the roots of television ("A chimeric word which offends many classicists.") Alan Davies, whose ignorance of Pliny the Elder is only equalled by his conniving charm, regularly scores minus 20. "Have you ever felt your weapon's not big enough?" he asked Jo Brand after a losing duel with the prof. "No" said Brand briefly. She has never felt that anything about her wasn't big enough.

Scheduling is the art of not getting your teeth kicked in. **Rosemary and Thyme** (ITV1) has fled Sunday, dominated by the frightful giant, Michael Palin, and settled on Friday. Where, next week, they will run straight into the gently smiling jaws of French and Saunders. The clever money will be on French and Saunders who have already done ...

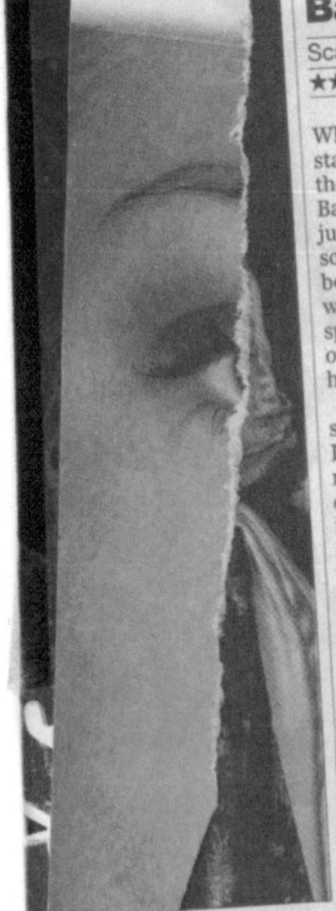

...der, and often brilliant play. In five taut ...nes, her characters ...ant ability to read ...er, and even less in ...nding themselves. ...mework for the play ...f fleeting and ...ymous encoun... lonely, lost souls ...ta, a childlike ... has moved to ...et who she ...l, and in ...ions tries to ...borrowing ...itor to her ...he next. ...he thinks ...rown-up, ...l invites ...ly ...se she ... evokes these ...llisions beauti... ...g silence as power... ...as words, and brittle ...medy as deftly as tremen... ...ness. The emotional ... the

esreview

Specia... in the ...

WOULD he or wouldn't he? Twice recently Pete Doherty, former Libertine and eager consumer of crack and heroin, has been billed to play London with his new band, Babyshambles. Twice he failed to appear. Last night, starting only two minutes late and finishing only one minute after curfew, his timing was almost Kraftwerkian.

He is, it transpires, worth caring about after all and not just because, with his puppy eyes and falling-down trousers he more resembles a lost boy desperate to be mothered, than a drug monster forever in search of Pakistan's finest. What, you suspect, this vulnerable manchild really needs is strong people around him rather than feral hangers-on.

Confused by any acclaim, he responded to the baying mob who were more ambulance chasers in search of a car crash than audience, by giving a little of what they wanted, leaping into them twice (once from the speaker stacks),

POP

Babysh...
Scala, N1
John Aizle...

before em... bloodied.
Elsewhe... flexible, s... band incl... an astoni... drummer, down, ex... elegantly nodded o... Libertine... turbocha...
Midway changed ... known fo... Dove's 19... Fallen) e... inaudible and duet ... gorgeous, composed Heart, the instinctiv... and Lee H... make rec... become t...

...and hail from a council estate in Hull. Meet The Paddingtons – ...real voice of youth culture

29 October 2005 NME 31

...first, now at NME.COM ...debut album...
"The camps... it," says Tom. "We were ... camp here?" Then, when it ... 10 tents ...

s
r

and

lined
larke,

led

a and
ne
a
Did.
ood
n (best
One
them

none
n the
elf-
. Your

natra
n they

Angela Lubrano

All puppy eyes and falling-down trousers: Pete Doherty at the Scala

George Jones and Tammy Wynette.

Mostly though, Doherty unveiled his Babyshambles repertoire. The current single Killamangiro was an under-produced example of where they might go, but much more indicative was the spellbinding Fuck Forever, a nihilistic anthem (albeit one not destined for saturation airplay) and Doherty's first claim to greatness.

They left with dignity, but without an encore. Such was the evening's intensity, it would have been superfluous. If — and nobody should underestimate just what a big "if" this is — Doherty can resist pharmaceutical temptation, he will be special. It's as simple as that.

The perf
to Baroq

NO FEWER than three sumptuously refurbished classical venues are open to the public this month. The Wigmore Hall, looking more elegant than ever, reopens on Saturday, while the restored glory of Hawksmoor's masterpiece, Christ Church, Spitalfields, can be experienced just over a week later.

Last night the managers of several leading chamber orchestras were checking out London's latest concert venue: Cadogan Hall, near Sloane Square. Built 1904-7 as the First Church of Christ Scientist, it has a Byzantine exterior, now enhanced to surreal effect by blue lighting, with a cool, almost functional interior.

Cadogan Hall is a very welcome addition to the London concert scene. As a medium-sized venue (900 seats) with a generous stage area, it is ideal for chamber or Baroque orchestras. Even from the worst seats in the house, under the gallery overhang — as I can personally vouch — the sightlines and acoustics are both good. The individual lines of the trio sonata in the Brandenburg Concerto No 5 in D, played by Stephanie Gonley, William Bennett

an
en
in
ba
F
so
an
if la
Engl
Orch
Bach
half b
but w
express
or rhytl
was true
Seasons:
work had
élan and s
pictorial e
the summ
vivid, but th
articulation
bear by the Be
Baroque grou
lacking.

Cadogan Hal
perfect — th
area is a di
provides
resoung ver
appe of Londo
hea

as anyone who's hitched

will be on French and Saun-

The Returns

racing across London with slim Jim at the wheel of Gills motor. Clara is in town and all that entails. She cheers me up I will say so. Nice to see you Miss C ... where you been?

Well mr man of magnitude idiosyncrasity its marvelous to see you as always. We are sitting quite close and writing through a shifting sitting non silence. My plans in London will all be clear in the next few months – promise!

Remember Peter, everyone wants a bit of you but dont give yourself away

Sex, + love is special and I wish you happiness, I wish you <u>true love</u> So dont do the silly slag x

What u up to?

The ~~coronet~~ stands before us drizzly London 1.00 am, fans shiver by the river awaiting returns. I'm to dart in the back door for the anti fascist shin dig.... I pick up a few hours after I left off. Back at Gillville with

I lost all ability to be nice I think, Im sorry x

This interruption that lies before me sums up the 'something' that is partly in the state of Arcadia. 'Rotton' might be a better wo—

...and hair from a council estate in Hull. Meet The Paddingtons – real voice of youth culture

"The campsites ... it," says Tom. "We were like, camp here?" Then, when it goes

↑ flyers picked up by 15 yr old meself from the Arcadia Centre, on one of my melancholic meandering round Birmingham as a lonely weekend busking boy eating cheap rolls & spending pennies round muses on plastic jackets + the TLS.

s to pi

[redacted]

Dear Peter Doherty,

Thank you for changing something for m
+ view things. I heard 'What a Waste
night I had a dream where the words w
wall and they floated out the window + fille
that THE LIBERTINES were special, + I

I love The Kinks, The Beatles, Bob Dylan, The Velv
Iggy Pop, The Rolling Stones, The Sex Pis
Ella Fitegerald, Bob Marley, Little Richard, but I

there at the time of the
missed it. That all
you gave me + load
somthing to be genuin
the pit of our stoma
Babyshambles are equa
Astoria to see you, but
but I still want to see Ba
you, especially the Ba
at our disapointmen

You have also inspired me to, pick up my guit
I learnt were 'Albion' and Music When the Li
brilliant as he always plays your songs on his guita
be king. which he has on repeat) I get yours
curtan call and Arcady. I hope that maybe one
had is too good to loose, but good luck with wh
with music that gives me a full blown emotional
excitement or just tears (at how good it is), you ar
+ your every thing Good about The English. ke
cunts who revel in every miskake you make
You probably get a kazillion letters lik

The Paddingtons –
voice of youth culture

it," says Tom. "We were like,
camp here?' Then, when it
10 tents

[redacted], February 2005

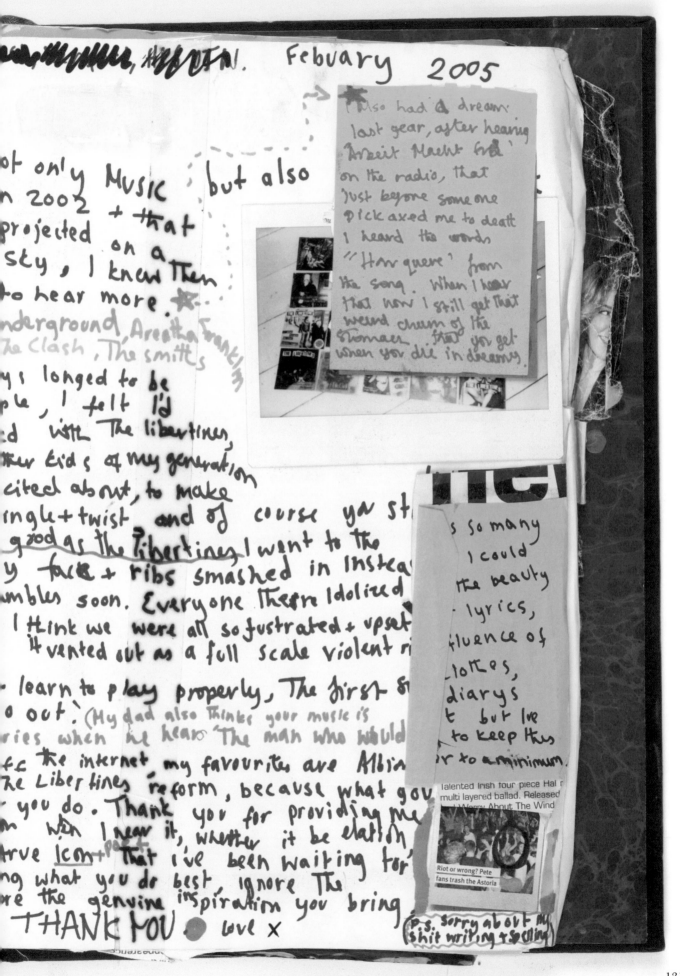

ot only Music but also
n 2002 + that
projected on a
sky, I knew then
to hear more.
nderground, Aretha Franklin
he Clash, The smiths
ys longed to be
ple, I felt I'd
d with The libertines,
ther kids of my generation
cited about, to make
ingle + twist and of course ya st
good as the Libertines I went to the
y face + ribs smashed in instea
mbles soon. Everyone there idolized
I think we were all so justrated + upset
it vented out as a full scale violent ri
learn to play properly, The first s
o out. (My dad also thinks your music is
ries when he hears 'The man who would
fc the internet my favourites are Albi
he Libertines reform, because what go
you do. Thank you for providing me
n when I hear it, whether it be elation
true Icon + poet that I've been waiting for
ng what you do best, ignore the
re the genuine inspiration you bring.
THANK YOU. love x

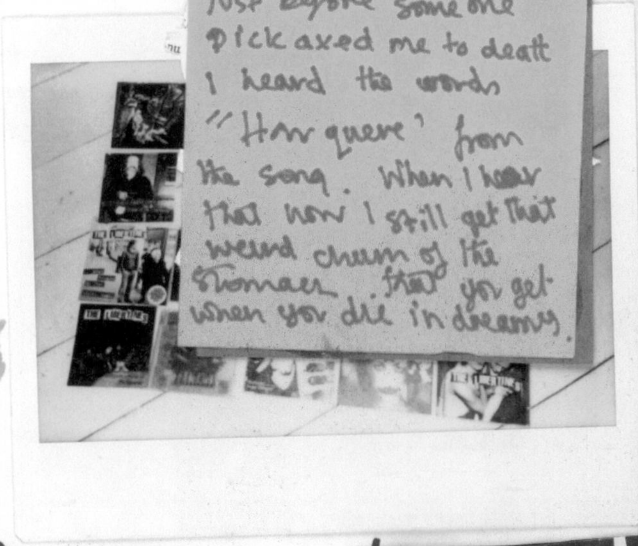

* I also had a dream
last year, after hearing
'Arbeit Macht Frei'
on the radio, that
just before someone
pick axed me to death
I heard the words
"How queer" from
the song. When I hear
that now I still get that
weird churn of the
stomach that you get
when you die in dreams.

s so many
I could
the beauty
lyrics,
fluence of
clothes,
diarys
t but I've
to keep this
r to a minimum.

Talented Irish four piece Hal
multi layered ballad. Released
Worry About The Wind

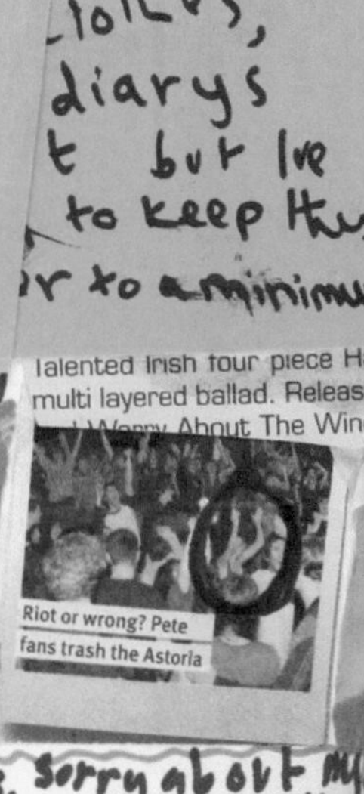

Riot or wrong? Pete fans trash the Astoria

P.S. Sorry about my shit writing + spelling

diletantes fantasy

Something has been brewing in the past couple of years that easily beats all of the 'Indie' with a capital corporate 'I', career-driven boredom merchant bands who ceaselessly populate our airwaves. It is a small unnamed scene which has largely revolved around a small little backstreet club in London called 'The Rhythm Factory'. Though there have been many important players in this scene one figure has dominated throughout and that figure is one Peter Doherty. Yes you all know him, even your Gran is aware of him but maybe not for the best of reasons. Pete Doherty is many things to many different people. To his fans he is a Galton and Simpson, Chaz n' Dave influenced, romantic poetry reading dilettante of the highest order to others he is no more than a tabloid martyr. Doherty reminds us of the age old values of punk rock dandyism as made famous by the likes of Joe Strummer and The Clash. Indeed former Clash lynchpin Mick Jones even produced his albums for The Libertines and a whole new generation discovered the aesthetic joys of the trilby and the porkpie hat (though enough now, its becoming a fashion). Stoke-on-Trent is part of the story too and this is where Doherty's new band Babyshambles comes into it. On Wednesday 21st April Babyshambles brought a slice of rock n' roll history to Stoke venue The Underground. If the Rhythm Factory is his first home then The Underground is his second. He has played there three times now but none of those times has yet to match the first. The 21st April gig was notable for its national headline grabbing post-gig riot. Libertines fans are an excitable bunch and these 'stylish kids in the riot' proved so unruly as to cause the gig to be pulled towards the end of the night and as the security attempted to shepherd away a crowd that refused to leave it was left to Pete (and his erstwhile Libertines partner Carl Barat, making a guest appearance that night) to take the crowd outside and to continue the gig in the car park. This gig was pivotal in many ways. At the time Babyshambles seemed more of a side project for Pete and not as big a concern as The Libertines but now the tide was starting to turn. Babyshambles played Stoke again within a week and then they began to tour as The Libertines started to fold.

Stoke …
band before a …
results and if you've …
Babyshambles gigs in Stoke, …
again on October 4th (get your tickets, …
fast). Also look out for the new Babyshambles sing…
'Killamangiro' out soon. Enjoy…

Peter Doherty is taller than you think he wears a trilby style hat which tops off his usual Dickensian urchin style dress and he is in a constant state of apparent distraction. Though I am initially quite annoyed by his constant air of detachment I recognise it as part of his charisma and I have to say, find it endearing by the end of the interview, it certainly works on stage too. I hand him a letter from myself and the other Kiosk members proposing how we'd like to make the interview into an artistic collaboration at a later date and he reads through it nodding in recognition at some of the conceptual artists listed therein. On coming across the figure of Pete Doherty my first thought had been - Is he attempting to pull off an intellectual pose or is he for real? With this in mind, I ask him if he remembers the old Smiths song 'Cemetery Gates', he does and he proves it by bursting into a quick rendition of part of it. Echoing Morrissey's lyrics I ask him: "Whose side are you on? Keats's and Yeats's or Wilde's?". "Verlaine's" he answers quickly and quietly and from then on I am in no doubt that this boy is really a true artist (for any Move readers who aren't in touch with old school French Romantic poetry - shame on you, go and look it up).

Remix became co-editors and partners in Movemag at a time when the local and national dance scene (as we'd known it for almost 10 years) was in its final death throes. It wasn't clear what would emerge as the new and most vital … the city at the time and we investigated … issues championing the … develo…

For that reaso…
band …

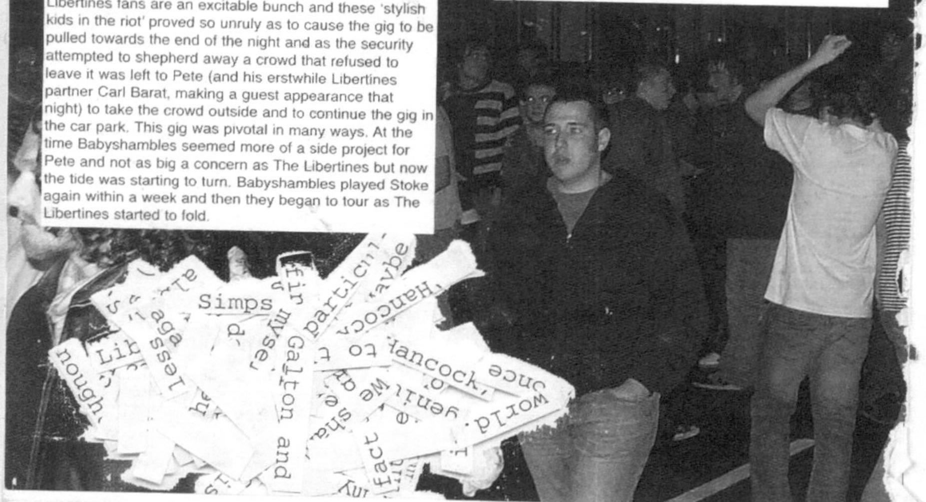

"Nothing is more precious than the grey song where the indistinct meets the precise" (Paul Verlaine from the poem "The Art of Poetry")

This might make a nice epigram for Doherty's whole persona. Like Verlaine himself, Doherty appears to lead, what some might term, a rather 'unsavoury' yet romantic existence. Take a look at his Babyshambles website (www.babyshambles.net), download the music that he generously and heroically offers for free and more to the point read his message-board and his Books of Albion - the term he uses for his e-journals, the books are a kind of online catharsis, if Verlaine could have discovered the delights of 'blogging' it may well have resembled Doherty's musings as one part of him watches in enraptured, impotent horror as the other slips into degradation. The prime reason behind the collective interest in Doherty's mental and chemical state arises from his own obsessive interest in it. He intensively lives his own poems and songs, or is that his songs and poetry reflects his life? We're not really sure and that's why he intrigues us. We asked him if his whole Albion myth is just a persona or if it means more to him than that?

"It's not a persona. I was very much isolated all the time; it's just the world I lived in. It just comes from my imagination. Just cellotaping together loads of dilettantes fantasies and see if you can actually live the poetry that you write".

He lives in that grey area between the indistinct and the precise, it comes through in his work, his live performances and it is even present when you meet him in person. As I have already noted he is detached and appears not to hear you but in fact he responds to everything, it is a dandyish mixture of arrogant posing and courteous politeness. You can never quite tell whether he wants to answer a question or not. "What do you make of Alan McGee?" he is asked and he swiftly replies "Well I don't make any money out of him". We move on but he suddenly decides to answer the question – "Well he's let me down hasn't he. He's managing the band and letting 'em play without me. Alan McGee said I'd be a millionaire if I put (the songs) "What Katie Did" and "The Man who would be King" on the (new Libertines) album, so we did…" he trails off tellingly, once again in his own world. We shamble on and while myself and 'Shambles drummer Gemma play noughts and crosses (deadlock no less), Pete and my fellow Kiosk co-conspirator talk Tony Hancock, both agreeing to the genius of 'Hancock's Half Hour' with Pete taking a particular interest in the fact that the writers responsible, Galton and Simpson, met in a mental hospital. Maybe less prosaically my friend is concerned to find out whether Pete is a radio or a TV man, all important stuff I'm sure you'll agree – "for we want the nuance, not the colour, the nuance" (Verlaine again).

In the run up to this interview the common view of Doherty has shone through in all its paradoxical glory. While countless people, who upon learning that I was about to conduct this interview, blithely asked me questions such as: "Do you think he'll live long enough to be interviewed?" or "I've heard he takes seven million pounds (or some such other medically impossible and ridiculous figure) of heroin or crack a day, do you think he does?" they enquire.

the

… the Paddingtons –
…oice of youth culture

it," says Tom. "We were like, … camp here?' Then, when it … 10 tents …

UPTIGHT
PAGE
6
Carl Barât:
“I’ll love Pete ’til my dying day”
26 Arctic

POLICE
The Paddingtons
voice of youth culture

unite against fascism
STOP THE FASCIST BNP
020 7833 4916
www.uaf.org.uk
Pete
Fran
Pottsie
do U want a competition
2 see who can sit on
hill the longest

a council estate
the Paddingtons –
voice of youth culture
“The campsites
it,” says Tom. “We were like,
camp here?’ Then, when it

The Paddingtons
voice of youth culture
it," says Tom. "We were like,
camp here?' Then, when it

of the lunatic
INGe

ANTHER
2/6
18th-century England,
a lusty, brawling isle . . .
I, LIBERTINE
FREDERICK R.
EWING
seething in ferment
in an age of
spectacular
abandonment
torments
in the
night
I'm righ
wrong
me
all in
all

Junkie Doherty
Junkie Pete t
KATE'S JUNKIE
Junkie Pete
ADDICT
PETE
JUNKIE
PETE IS
JUNKIE PETE

Wolfeman is along the lines of saying that I'm in love with [redacted] (whom malicious gossiples have been saying I tried to bag off with)

This is dangerous & darkening suggestion, intent of malicious I suppose, with a healthy innocenty smile accompanying his words.

Even so, he overshadows his intolerable intrusions into my composed affairs with a perfectly comforting understanding of misery & grotesque agonies imbedded in the soul.

we drove to Kent together & in a tiny churchyard watched a field of deer in the early morning sun.

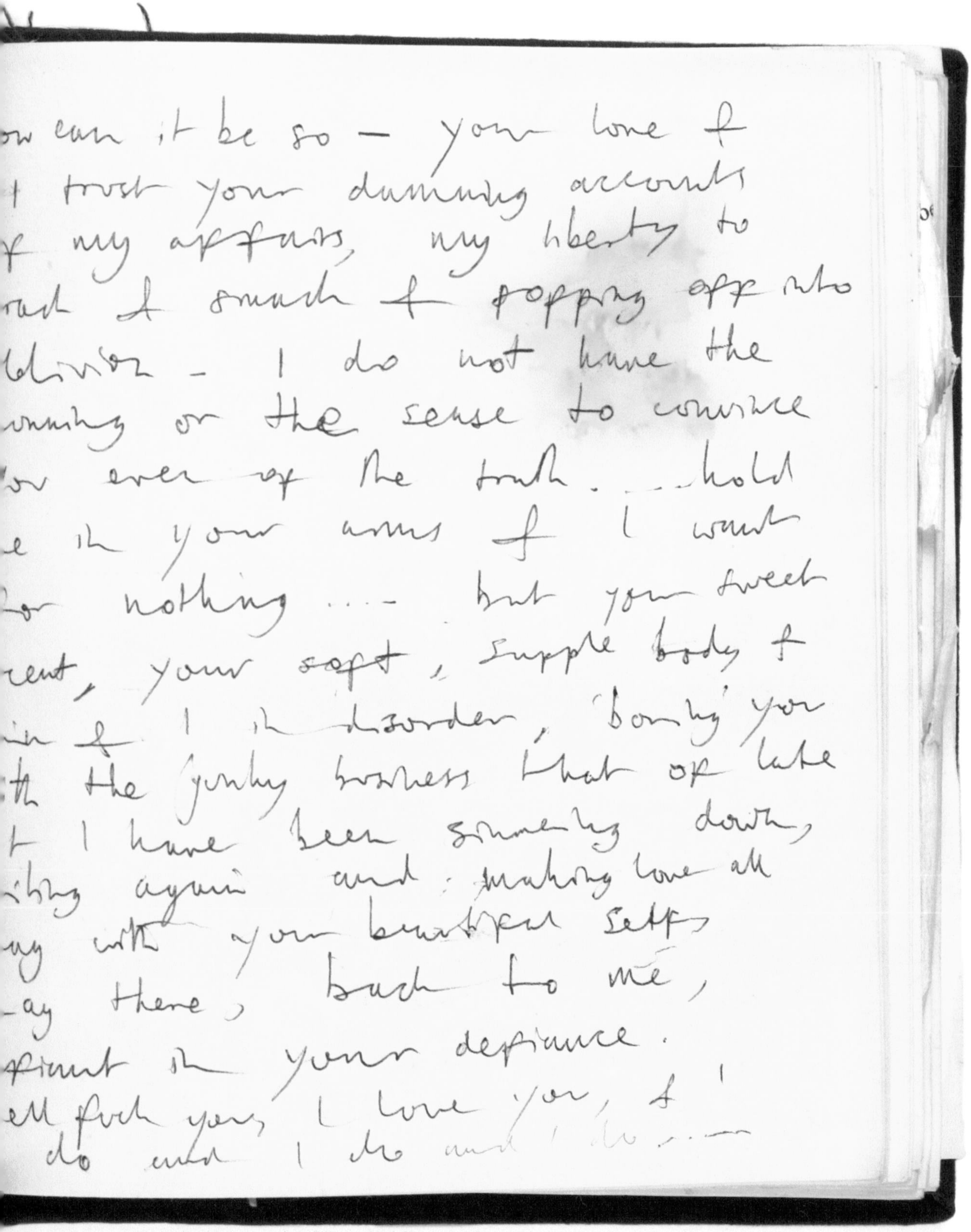
ow can it be so — your love &
t trust your damning accounts
f my affairs, my liberty to
rash & smash & popping off into
blivion — I do not have the
unning or the sense to convince
ou even of the truth … hold
e in your arms & I want
or nothing …. but your sweet
cent, your soft, supple body &
in & I in disorder, 'boring' you
th the funky business that of late
t I have been simmering down,
ising again and making love all
ay with your beautiful selfs
ay there, back to me,
fiant in your defiance.
ell fuck you, I love you, & I
do and I do and I do ——

I ask Keith the
date. It is
the 7th of
April. It's
3.48 in the
morning.
Who remains:
Pandy Keith,
Keith,
& myself.
Safe
am I ...
Keith being my
bodyguard & Pandy are

ear to ear . . .

now who will buy my beautiful roses
who will buy my beautiful songs. . . . .

Cant show no decorum
Spilt my heart out on the
forum, was
like a snapshot of the most
tragic ~~fotos~~ day . . . .

shall I tell you my story
the treachery so bores me . . . .
Carl & Magee both promised me
it would not happen this way . . . . .

Carl is kept sedated
to the front man elevated
while Magee does all he can
to ruin the band & keep me out the w
In an industry ~~of~~ fools mouthmen
~~&~~ ghouls

if you're not a puppet or a puppet you

the only phone for miles rings. I answer -
it's Kate. To try and explain
the wonder, blunder and blind
folly of my conduct would be
to class myself as a master in
this writing lark. I never could
My voice like a throat in a frog
my lungs shattered, heart battered
at peace was I ... with Keith....
minesweeping and having a tidy
The darling even made the fucking
bed ... dear oh lordy be it's been
a ride ride ride this time round
Anyway.. the folly on the phone.
talking in cracked tongues
all she says is 'what?'
and all I says is things like
'Kissle dont have a pop. between
yourself & melody you've stitched me
right up...'
So you see the predicament it is
to be thus a neak of fracture
As light becomes day in Wales....
as light becomes day

See again them again

Theres another picture on in an hour but your surroundings change the same so much. Harbour yourself and maybe straighten your back. I am in Belfast we sat at a bus stop awhile, beside a barricade and the advertising hoarding that harboured a wasteland. Patches of grass and rubble stacked like promises. Nothing was calculated, thank fuck for the thought at once and after waiting a while. I was sat up on the metal and saw my reflection in the scratched plastic of the stop. She used her phone just to let you know the memorial think but I'm in love so before later when I away.

On the news corpses are being dug up all over the country & the Americans are trying to hold things together, shifting like oil their grip on the policing of the world

watch the wind for it is
restless. Alan Wass rocks back
and forth. his head facing
the carpet. hidden by his
wild mop of tangled hair.

coming down are we from a
hell of weekend or so in
Ireland. Belfast & Dublin
hosting a shambles hatch
of horrors & glory.
Drug psychosis, town bus
carnage, still harbour
waters in the close light of
dawn. Happenny bridges &
champagne breakfasts, crisps,
& rummaging in bins.
~~Jimmy~~, Horse, Brandy &
Magowan's whizz

Was a joy I know to
see Kate her self so
full of wonder & splendour
is her self. In a world

LE GLASGOW STRANGLER STRIKES

Katie England & Bobby G explain things away.

Dear Sir

Soz about the carnage but don't get the hump with Kate, it was her mate Katie ~~Bobby's~~ girl who really went loopy and trashed the joint.

Love

Peter Roberts

P.S. Dear Sir — infact I was the innocent amongst a group of drunkeness! Things got out of hand, please forgive their extravagant behaviours. Its an extravagant place.

DEAR SIR, WE HAD A FUCKING RIOT LAST NITE IN YOUR BEAUTIFUL HOTEL IT WAS A BLAST, THANKS. FOR THE UPGRADE TO THE OPULANT MANSION, SOME COCAINE ON ROOM SERVICE WOULDN'T GO AMISS - COULD SAVE YOU A FEW MIRRORS ETC, YOURS B. GILLESPIE

in a strange & hypnotic world
of paradoxes it occurred
that it would look bad
to court marshall 2 fellas
so they got medals of
honour. Similarly last
night after festivities or
rather derangement of the
senses in Kates Cannes hotel
room ... mirrors were smashed
& I covered my love &
the whole room in bloody
Mary

well now we're on the
flight back to London
from Nice & that was the
first 'holiday' I've had
in so long, well, since
Prison really. Now the
Boeing 767 glides us
home through a fantasy
of clouds and summer
sky. The sea of red weddingtermen

in the office

Jim mouths the words of 'he who laughs last laughs longest' responding to [illegible] whatsits footage of the ongoing onslaught he can frown a smile upon to remind of the frequency I turn away from him in mid-conversation.

It must occur to him from time to time or so that I must soon take it & run ie: hotfoot it into Arcady further more ... to totally follow my heart & the melody of the stars & in those calamitous & divine betrayal of either: my heart or my fate?

Such questions meddling models from Montmartre (or near) assault my night with and early on!

Either way I had a fine old map with Ali down Birch Lane yesterthedas bowling & strolling & swallowing through

a patter of tiny feet
remind you of your own again
& ~~am~~ you alone again or ?
well now
the walls are white and
invisible
if you do not forget
the wishes
7 fishes lay on the chopping board
across the wayfare was a
lemon & a knife. A brush
of salt ~~on~~ the slabby floor

a chair squeaks wooden across
the floor slabs

Butter pervades the kitchen
& a mother is in the hall
days stutter in the sunlight
& my heart flutters so in the
voices of a summer
evening

Box Office Tel: 0870 112 1967 V.A.T. No. 677 9797 38

in the birdsong lullaby of
a summer morning I lull
I tiptoe to the window,
around which is wound
a noble tangle of leaves
and - oh glorious - red,
white & blue roses ....
You lay sleeping under
bear-cat, the softest of
soft fur white polar silky
bed covers ... I kiss your
sleepy head & shoulders,
and I'd kiss your shadow
& your shadows reflection...
although if you're still
vampiring it up you'll not
have a reflection my sweet.

I reach for your
hand & amidst your
stirring & regular
breathing your arm is
restless & your
fingers have to grasp
for You <u>are</u> asleep
though even as I
write this you
stretch and scratch
& wiggle now &
sigh ... & settle
again. I kiss
your face, shoulders
& nestle with many
sweet salty tasting kisses.

V.A.T. No. 677 9797 38 Box Office Tel: 0870 112 1967

Kate my love Kate my sweet
I scrawl at dawn & cant
wait for patience :.....
I would betray my fate
before I would my heart
in fact I'd betray the whole
world & all in it before
betraying my heart ....
I mean to say
You have my heart
although now you are kicking
me in your sleep & so
so you dont love me ....
oh but you do : say 'I love
you so' and my senses are
ransacked, raised to cinders all
[illegible] already should to or fro

Senses deranged maybe
but no numbing or
narrowing of the mind
can strip my soul of its
orchestra that pipes up
in crescendo when you
say you love me, and
in my heart I am inclined
to trust you & thats all
my dreams you toy with or
indeed fulfill.

1

ah me

I do crave the loneliness' grave – be away with it once and for all – I do yearn for my love and lovelorn shall I be until she awakens me from this torpor with sweet kisses & how's your father. Yes come the coppers and carry off the loneliness, less all days are known only for the boney rap of vice on my window and the pony and trap that is the snap, cackle & plop of the papparazi & the ilk in the rotton milk media that sours the ~~milk~~ sweet soup of ours and cuts down towers to size of mice and men are pecked by two faced diseased hens shuffling their weird trotters along the all the way like so many shit ~~shovelling~~ lumpihy totters hoof of haunted yesterdays

May the farce not outlive you nor your body's will to leap boundaries and burst through barricades into brave new borderlands and sword of seventh in your hand hack down the tangle of traps and thickets full of head fuckers for all they'll do is do ya.

Tell doom to 'do one'
if you're on for another reckless
turn on the rivers ~~[illegible]~~ apocalypse
of rocks & rushing waters
the throat burnt up dry as you
nearly drown in frozen over tides
Trust yourself like metal trusts rust:
in a simple formula

Listening ears up pinched to an old
old old demo from Odessa days

PAY THE LADY
LUST OF THE LIBERTINES
BRECK ROAD LOVER

If you're lonely you may
hear a voice through the ages
from some lungs full of scent
of heather and ancient song
pissed out of his head watching
a young mother plait hers &
her daughter's hair

V.A.T. No. 677 9797 38 Box Office Tel: 0870 112 1967

when even I saw her herself
(very self) not some Superhuman
fantasy of the very age
although that does help
when young hearts have
innocent (?) yearnings for
the shape, sort (!), sweetness (shit
scary) splendour, splashed all
over the mainstream media — immediacy
immediate, mediate, diet — the Albion
diet never failed me, but
I see from her writing I have
failed her.

MARTELL
VS

well sorrow & despair declare
themselves ... well, they're
checked out & fervour
love & delight (and poss
exploding elephants) reign
the day
all day I could follow
her gaze like the world
but the sons of gods'd
have it tough not to control
themselves with her there
how can I throw myself
into her when she's off
so often & my tough &
tough foot stir appall
I know still the music
plays & so

ever

never seen anything
like it in my life
she's amazing dancing
rolling her shoulders
in her cut up dress
I'm so wrong I know
but if she loves me
I'll scream with joy
an eternity of
shy shadows glancing
at myself I can't
cry for numbness
but my days I'm
prone to believe
and watching her
dance la like f
Tika rivers deep
mountains high
all that matters and
all that will ever

You have touched my
heart and soul, little
fucker. I wish you would
ring on my door now so
I could kiss you again
and float away. You make
me high, my sweet, my
skin shivers and longs
to be held by you.

(day after, to self

nominally in disorder / in a fashion
commonly wont in this pressing matter not
of unignorable pressure – abrasive selfish
conversations with the blank dirt that
glues the corners of my backwards minds
altogether outside ~~the high walls~~
levering the face off with the sticky
oil of grey tears. They dry and up
the sense out of the skin's mask. In
past lives I was blank .... actually deadly
sleepy and convinced by my corrupt reasoning
that I was wide awake and ready to
break into a running jump. As it turns out
I fell off a small step and ruined
my jumper.
Oi... idle reader, perch the dogs bark
on a silly sentence, fence off the
offenders and drug & drown the
nearest & dearest that might officially
complain and rupture bike force
thank you and very good night.
Don't drive the car away it is
planted just now with bomb like
to be called – the ~~car~~ I mean – primed
or what was it? Rigged........

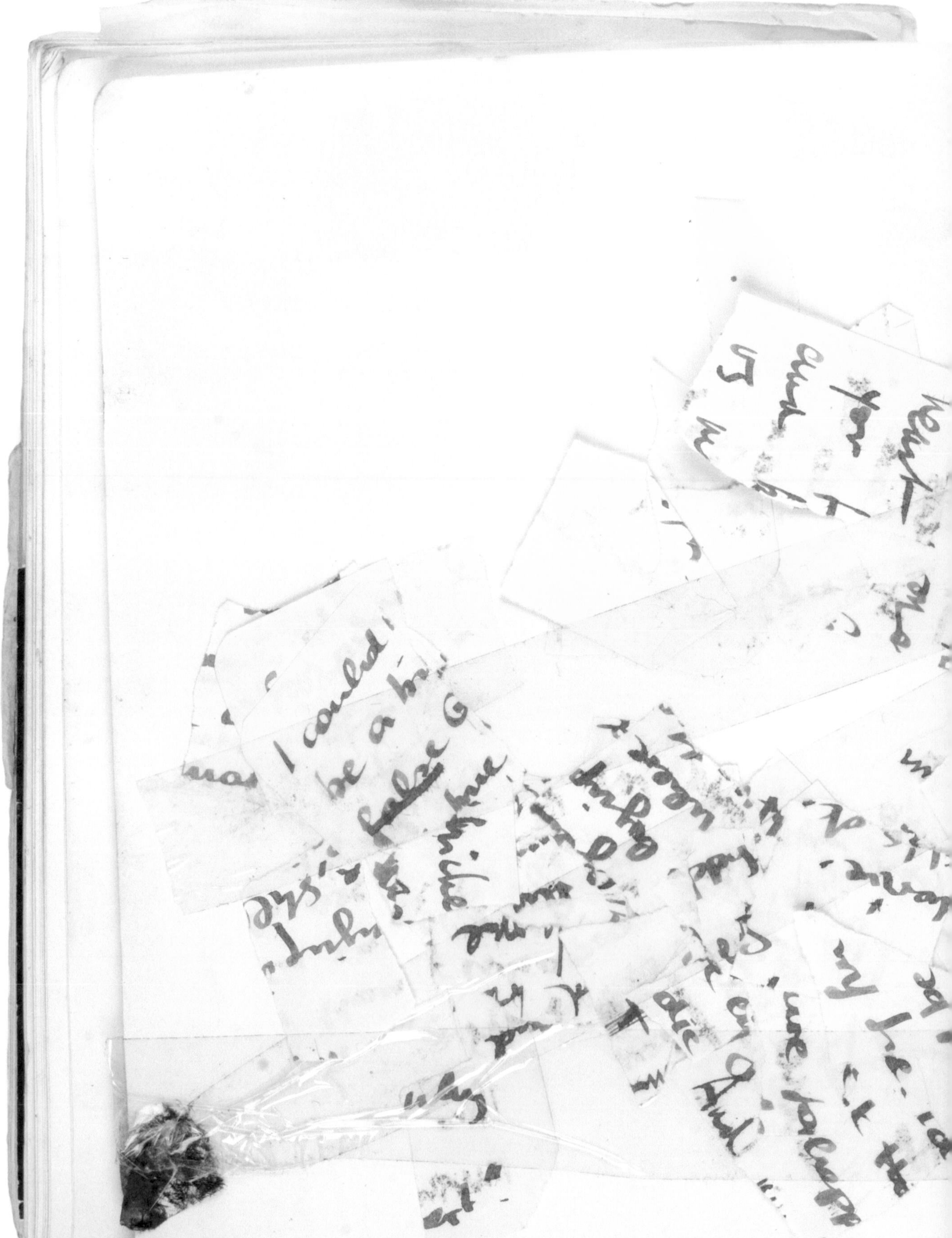
I could
be a
false

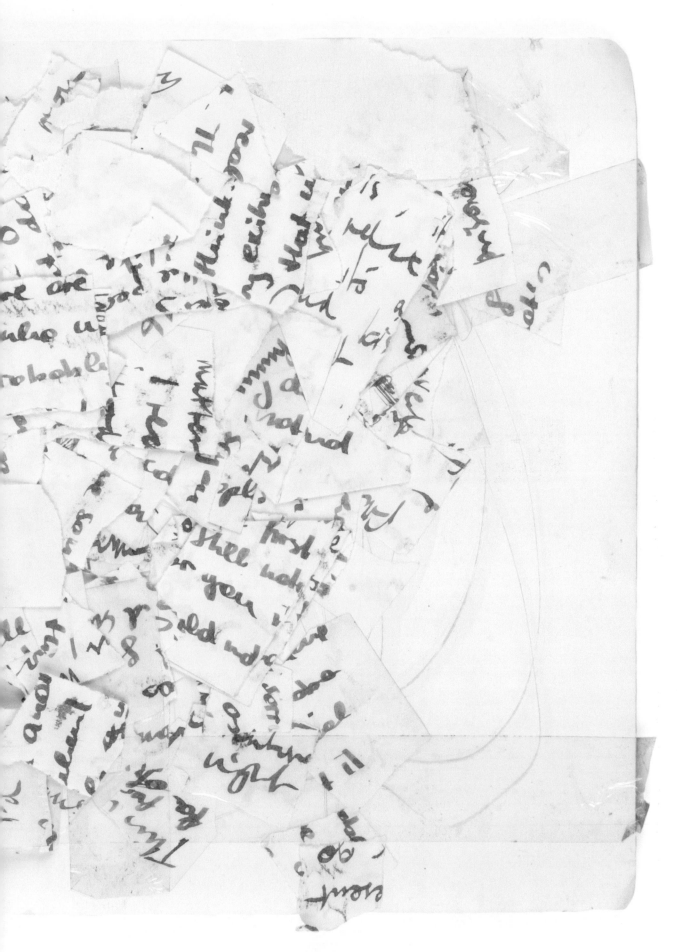

YEAH

WRIT IN CRUEL HAND

white
lite
straight to the
heart of the matter
my 2 mil served on
battered copper platter
coz the wealth aint
the heart of the
matter its the
poverty that feeds
the fat get fatter
the poverty that breeds
signs & receives government
dirt deeds designed to keep
the poor on the floor

You are light in pink
slips on summer mornings
flexing vodka + tonics (I
hope it is plural) in what
we may say is your air
of disgust for me, you have
just

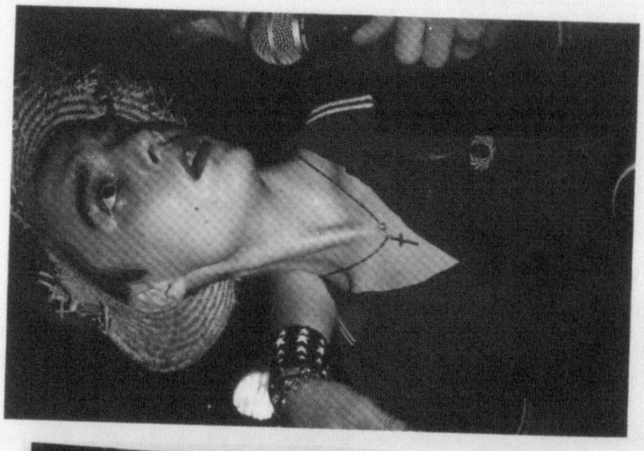

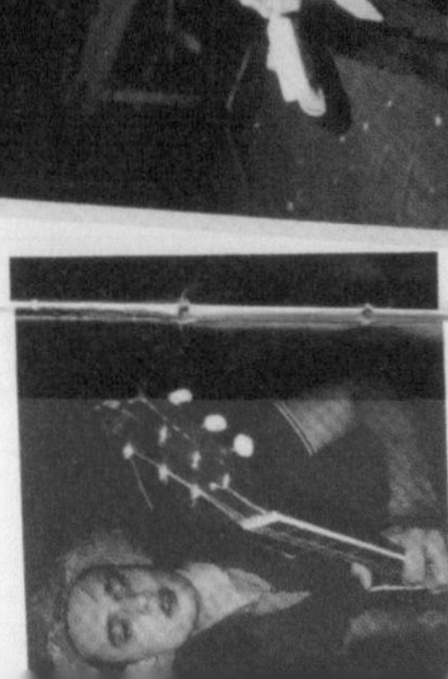

…モデルのケイト・…で逮捕された際に…ダメな恋人」と…ップされたことは…けとなって、わが…ったることとなっ…ホだ。だが、不思…き散らして刑務所…ている彼の姿は、…・ローゼズでおな…ス・ドラッグ・ロッ…スタイルとは異…規範を嘲笑する、…せる——「セック…ル」的な行動の根…ある。だが、ピー…エルトン・ジョン…は、クスリでへ…を買う。予告もな…を行う。逆にギグ…になる事も。バン…クビにする。ノ…

エルとリアムを怒らせる。デーモンを怒らせる。呼吸をするのと同じくらい自然に、触れるものを無茶苦茶にしていくピート。結果として社会の規範が侮辱されたり、大人が逆上したりはするが、当の本人はあくまで無自覚で、罪悪感も希薄だ。反逆の意志にすら縛られない、この危うい無防備さは、過去の問題児たちの系譜には見られない。

■聴き手の魂を解放する「絶対の自由」

ピート自身にしても、かつてリバティーンズという「帰る場所」があった頃は、まだここまでではなかった。そこには彼を正気の社会につなぎとめる、カールという対等の存在がいたからだ。しかしリバティーンズがなくなった今、ピートは、未整理の混乱した心をさらけ出し、本能が命ずるままに生きている。彼の作る音楽もまた、音楽的な批評の地点を離れ、純粋な一個人の魂をそのまま音にしたような、もろくて凄みのある表現に変質しつつある。今の無軌道な生き様を、いつまでも続けていく事は不可能だろう。遅かれ早かれ、年貢の納め時は訪れる。だが、少なくとも今この時、ピートを縛りつけるものは何もない。その無防備さ、無自覚さゆえに、社会や道徳が押し付ける窮屈な価値観から完全に自由でいられるピート。そんな彼だからこそ作ることができる美しい音楽に、人は抑圧された自己を託そうとする。どこまでも破天荒な彼を通して、大げさな言い方をすれば、人は自己の魂を解放しようとしているのだ。

HARD TO EXPLAIN 9

so did I stray to from the story? I reached the Ritz — in a necklace of chains my lover and fate drag me through Paris at the speed of wealth, through and to Hedi's do surpasses my surmise that has surprise and all manner of parading as but 2 carry on's. Paddingtons and Pet Shop Boys, Les Parisians and many an ancient or modern lover may I be seen to look looks into and equally eyes lock mine from a slide show of mostly meself and a gradually fached gig I may hay to shamelessly cop off with my love through 'til I do indeed stumble up and onstage and help Tom massacre one of my favourite songs of course

---

To shop local and avoid carbon emissions.... Screens leading identities up aerials and away from their manor. conduited means channelled and its a conduit we are devising to rechannel the conduited — 'no' no? 'open the conduit' up the morning up the postcode ideas flashing like sparked fellas in raincoats through my mindless ways. Glitter round the boundaries of E1 — every crack house in the hood will have a 1 to 5 star rating based on the quality of the bone that houses too — where they clean and chat. Likened to eating a privet hedge in order to get a line of speed. Goodness how tired eyes can't stay shut

Back to the story? Kate & I fucking and fighting all the way on the Eurostar until finally blood runs down my palm & up my head, and before I leg it to oblivion leaving her at the station calling me a this that & the other and a so-and-so (accompanied by hand gestures) and the dramatic exit just on queue as my deranged senses all aplume moving away from the flashing bulbs of the ninja papparazzi's and dear old Jimmy Mulford sticking a left hook right in the mush of one of the photographers — 'smack!' he

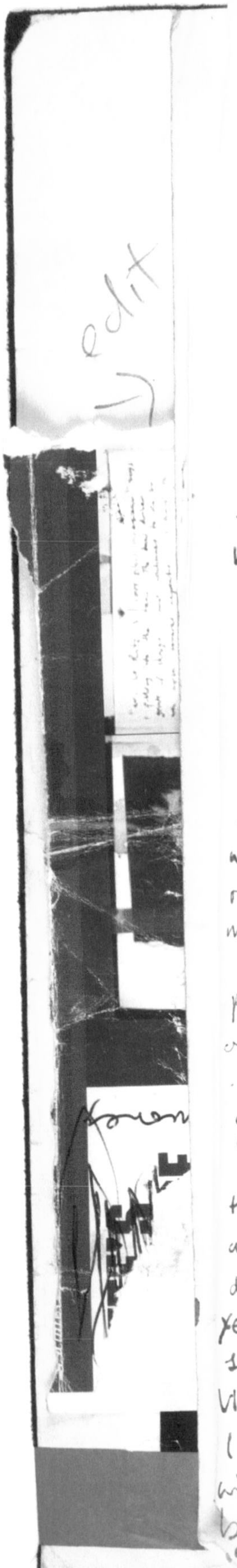

caught him a good'un I will say to meself. Hopefully there'll be no follow to the incident, given the shambles' run ins with the law of late and all the ill-luck that follows us about keener than stalkers.* Must make note to follow up myself given the pleasure & excitement I felt when James cracked the photographer one. cheered us both and I think my dear manager needed to release some tension here or there... of late the goodwill of Fate leads us not unto hell-in-a-handcart, but still to fuck-knows-where via temptation itself. Shambler's have we been, scene after scene, piping pinned and powdering noses on planes... debauching it at the airports all over Europe. Shunned at Mummerzoom shunned, paranoid, gunned down in the void betwixt heathens, dancing girls and this band and that band.

Back to now and a summer dawn rains down on London. E1 UK is the embroided Parka walking out the door and in again laden with newspapers full of tabloid mumble jumble about our exploits in Paris. Vaguely, surreally connected to the truth... red-top rags seem to have a new resolution: to write absolute shite about the 'troubled rocker' and his supermodel girlfriend. The words they put into my mouth ... honestly the cut, paste & twist of the gutter journalist: will they not desist this shit and give the pupple a miss. My vanity all in a twist. Ha! No stylist or publicist to protect poor Bilo in the shark infested waters of hell's canal. Oh mercy and the stench of grime and ruddy guts as assassins jackall and jostle in nasty packs about the cartoon character they have presented the numbed readers with ... hit & run, dumb down and down and down, until I get picked up by some saviour or other dusted down and up & away into Arcady, this time next year this lone salty tear that falls may yet reach the sea, drowning in rivers lost under London like Victoriana. Leaking oh my love, I was not waving I was drowning. To the merry tune of a fizzing wire mesh freebase pipey, my shadow shamefaced behind me, cor blimey, god blind me lest I see myself

whey dont kill me tommy god love me
what thrills me may kill me and bruised skies above me
temper the verse and dash on the workers
drink to the curse and dont forget to put ~~flower~~ gauze
flowers on my grave

steel roses & stone lilies
forget me nots & clematis, sunflowers & poppies all
fashioned out of wire mesh. carry on scraping....
'where the bee sucks there suck I
in the cow-slips bell I lie' Ariel says so, and a car
ariel snapped off do I use to gather ~~suck~~ the honey through the
machine neck & blaze into smoke to take & choke
my remaining mornings. Mourn I the tempest in
duller days .... indeed or they would not be duller days.
I do not feel any desperation, sat alone when I'm not
alone, because I'm just picking up the pen again since
my love blunted 'the end' where we begin, and the fever
returns me to the capital...... waters that do not flow
et in Arcady ego

'Nymphs & shepherds' demands the nymph (if I may)
of the shepherd, who to my dismay says
'Paki satyrs' though in jest I know
and so dismay has to go
and all comers, colours, sisters & brothers with
souls intent ~~set~~ on nowt but ~~peace wished~~
love or such for one another
→ it means something to me
even whispered as derision choruses up
and begrudgers run amok trampling the
scenery and turning hearts to stone

A strum through 'a fool there was' and the melody o'that
ol' number hitching a speeding up versional accident
spit on the tape or soundly but then I'm nonsense to
resist itself. Many ventures spring to mind and
arent I free of all things I must be free by now?

a third of the sorrow I repeat the fractured status
my chipped at mashed, peeled & boiled mindful of
melody I repeat the fractured status my fried thursday
weekens at the knees. Research from 1860 (?) testing
out Diamorphine on local people - became known as
heroin because the company traded on the strengthening
effect or 'heroic' feeling that those tested on described
Naturally the trial group became the first smackheads
and ended up collecting scrap metal to fund their
newfound habits ... and so became known as 'junkies'.
This is said to have happened in Germany, perhaps
during Bismarck's reign (that's yr skag so it's 3 yrs
fokin bald that youre)

da da da da da oi da da da da da oi
da da da da da da da
people go on and on and on and on and on
and on like they even know whats going on
into this world where we been drawn they kill you
before you're born and pawn your soul to be No. 1

From 'Skag & Bone man'

shiver down my cracked bone
have another line though
shivers up the back bone
tick up on the pipe bro

oзeh up ran & ran
scratching the envaged pages with the metal feather ~~feather shaped metal~~ nib
I reside in the stagnant tide of the afternoon
if your head is feeling ~~hollow~~ bombed
& they pissed all your dreams
and your ~~social~~ soul is finding [life lost]

more or less loss &
my heart laid bare
the way it comes across
that I do not care
feeling lost and badly dressed
more and more of less & less

why would I ~~be found~~ wait until
~~the waiting for~~ tomorrow when I've already seen
all ~~sorrow~~ that's in store

oh I'll beg steal & borrow & use any means [fair or foul]
to keep a-hold of all what I ~~sorrow~~ ~~[illegible]~~ chav's
oh I'd love to turn you on when you turn & turn
oh I know you say it's ~~so~~ dull or so for you
staring at me staring (at the) flam~~[illegible]~~
and when that's that and all I ~~have~~ know is the peach the spoon to adore
or stare at you, & hurting back you
all sirens ~~[illegible]~~ on the rocks rocks & bang while they mash up
all your heads & heart's once so pure
[head up in the dock] raise the kaboose, ~~light~~ the lecky leads a noose
She's got a ~~[illegible]~~ door that locks and ~~while~~ like you hang
they'll smash up
like the men outside the mosque gritting his teeth in prayer
bombs ~~the town~~ falling down around me
as I raise the kaboose, crack my skull

when you talk about your ~~brother~~ lover
since you walked out on each other

know I'm a mess me, ~~and that the~~ but when you test me & you
~~[illegible]~~ kiss and caress me
~~and then~~ I need for nothing more than
maybe some wine
e taste of my beloved is, vodka & ciggies

Worship &

why would you follow ~~whe~~ ~~You're already~~ ~~I've already been~~ him and then tear the sod from limbs to limbs

The entire London transport network has all but packed up this afternoon in the wake of today's bombings. Mick wanders up to the flophouse & says how the bomb has upset him 'dont like people blowing each others heads off' If it all kicks off in East London, i.e the 'intelligence agencies' point the finger at a particular terrorist group and Islamic passions

edit

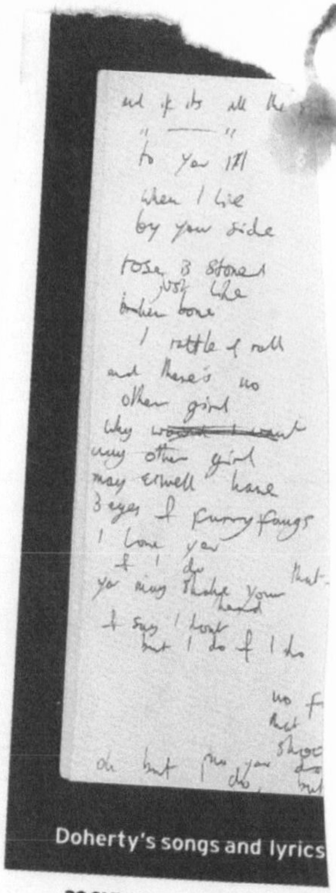

Doherty's songs and lyrics

20 OMM October 2005

METROPOLITAN POLICE SERVICE
Form 5090
Reason Stop D
Reason Search B
Outcome Code 1

"spend 2 hours
staring at
a fucking
Spoon"
1
2
3
Whack
edit

Oh so you are not here now and so I
greive the salty, sopping eventide with a
mess of feeling & reeling around the forest
clearing in time that tears afford me. Salt
blind I stumble into the night & pile
heartache upon confusions. Alas I am last to
understand my minds instructions

The staircase rattles to the stampede and out into
the night a dozen feet follow on each others steps.
Only one will open the gate, the last to be last

This is no sad plight - the lucky
seer of the blindity! Hark! Doth Purple
tread steadily upon the plank walkway?

The patience that time hath my mind taught
heaves me distraught ... my lungs heave in
foggy pipe-taut scripts of breath & the
London night is swallowed up by headache blackout

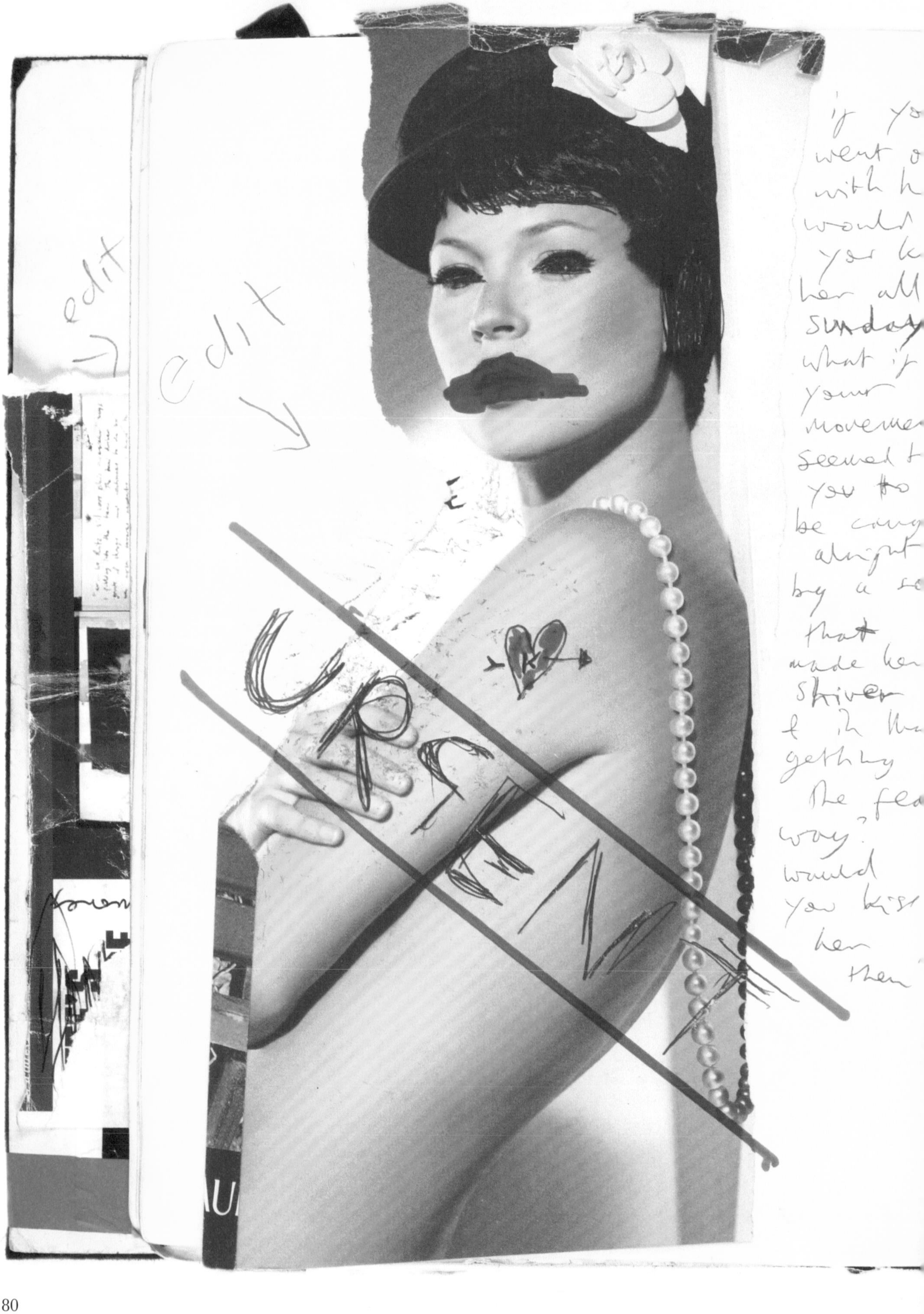
edit
edit
URGENT

he story

'oo stern you were on the turn with the turner

)nce time morning upon a start of a story's endle, I got a handle on the scandal of
ateness in love. Not being present still wouldn't bother the you know who that's
athered not by a stoned boned out rollin with half unto arcady and the rest…. Restless
ellmates, well-heeled hoodlums, no salesmen radiant palemen rastas casuals, crude-boys
nd photographers who try and look male.
Anyway back on the branch at Malinupalavas I was balancing for all of my worth (oi~)
nd trying to wake you up, editoresss, becausew oh you know some things like
eartsmindsmelodies musn't be corrupted or scratched faverouti r=e records
Riff from 'I feel fine'. But actually the fingy - ba

So and so said to such & so I said that there is
much of a murkness to the duchesses & old dears
that fill mad banqueting halls with their swine-like
ears. Hairy souped out conversations with the air
gestures that go spectacularly incomplete, like the
music on the bumper cars of the electrical circuit
winds down for the next lot of fairground freaks
my rotten guts clinging to the acid of itself
and crushing the time in bile. The label has
me off myself and I am bound to the
rain of love's bullet train that screams by me and
sends all my things flying till I'm in the
ditch soaked, cursing & crying my soul dry
of feeling, my senses fraying and my whole
...ve praying for god to give the ghastly gits
of hands of suffering a right pasting soon
enough couldn't be sooner. Or better still
soon ... my love to take me in her arms
and love me as my soul so desires.

edit

Norway mate

Sonic Yoof fella
introduced himself
& his wife
Jonny Headlock was on form
at the aftershow
kids etc spiel
Husky Wolfhounds in
Oslo ghetto brick pipes
Airport laughter paranoia
Pat sleeps, Mat weeps, & my implant
sleeps

backstage
carnage
Pat sleeps
with his
eyes open
fucked up
shit that.
I was talking
to him for
½ an hour
until Drew
pointed it out

SUNDAY MIRROR, *August 14, 20*

KATE: I DO

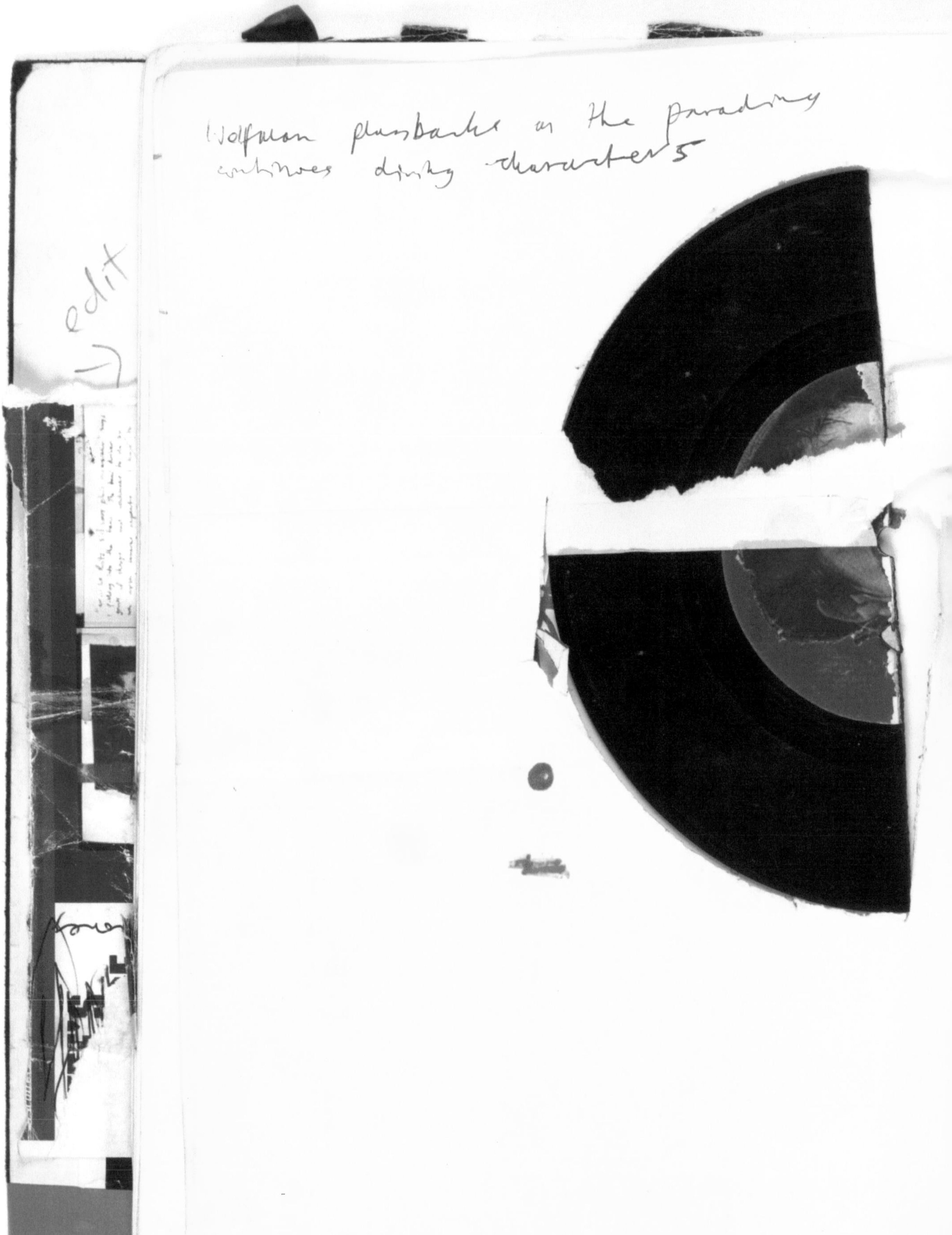
Wolfman flashbacks as the parading
continues during characters
edit

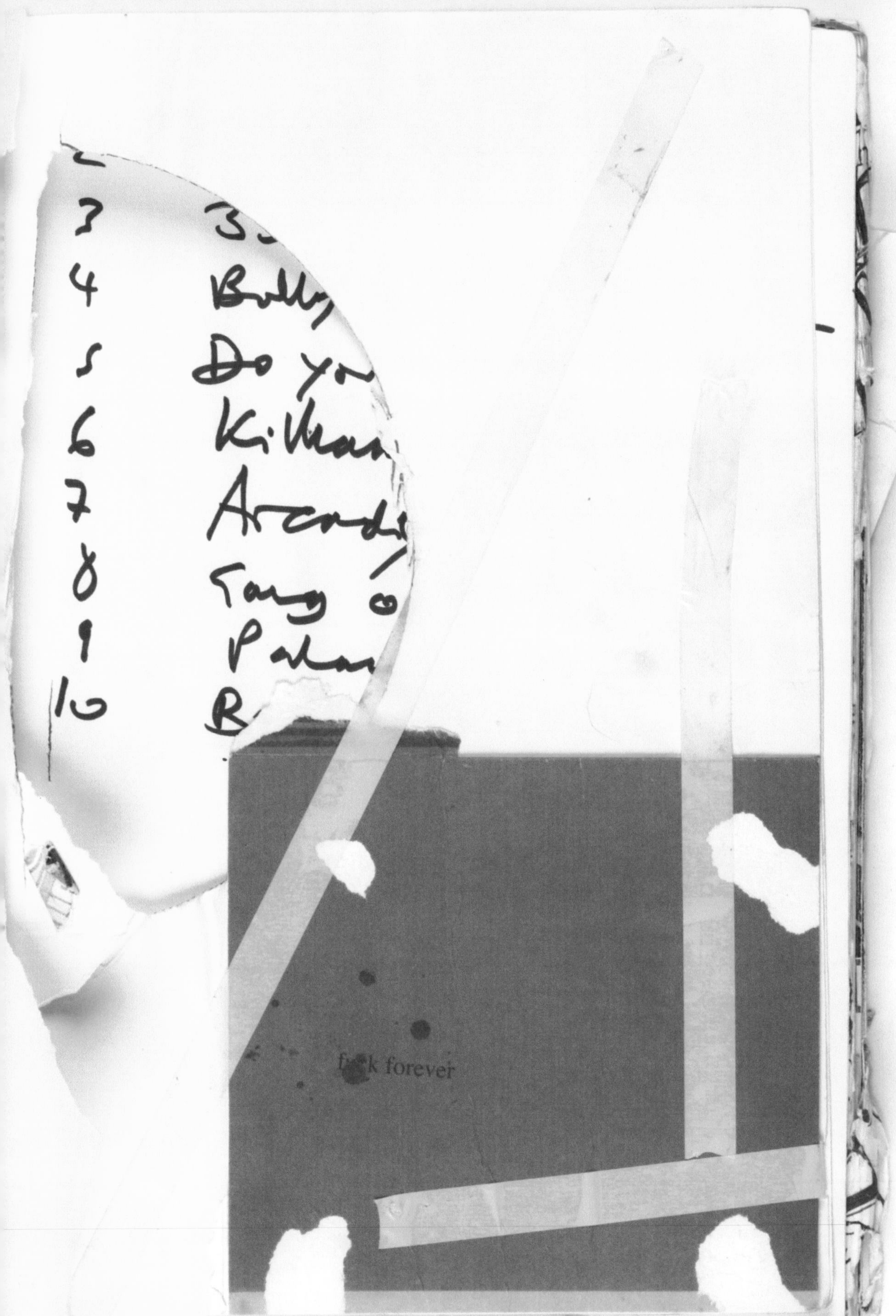
3
4
5
6
7
8
9
10
forever

Had a knees up at
Franny's after the
Manchester Academy
gig although Sonny
& Alan were rattling
their antlers like
the night as
blew the
out of the
Kaboose melted
sides
sweet souls
us in
dance &
roars
& family
all round
until the boys
off & Milky Blue-eyes
mob out

NYC September 12th 2005

towel around my wet hair head in bed anyway
ate in the afternoon. I must be deaf as I
couldn't hear the chinaman bringing in the
laundry. Dolls sing puss in boots on the sony
CD player. I'm in 606 at the Mercer, I suppose
I am awaiting my love, and in love I am.
have come with her across the Atlantic Ocean, and
whilst she works I walk & write & bathe & now
evening must come and with it decreasing pain
continues in the lower belly abdomen eastside. My
body is spitting out naltrexon bullets (5 down now)
25 to go. Today I strolled around New York
while, lost in the colours and threat & cut
of this cut throat gentle city. You never can tell
which, sirens blare here & there & there's a scene
in the street. Macho, aggressive voices threatening
to chop someone up. The whack of a ball against
a wall in the metal fenced park.

smack! we

edit

Doherty crashes out against the dressing room wall, Dundee, 23 September.

'come on .. you've got to get out of this room for at least an hour'

'why?'

Debris, ash, tin lids for egg plates, towels [illegible] wraps, snaps. Because I love you, as the soundly winds down and the night changes its name. My [illegible] is restless, endless energy, [illegible], [illegible] hips & shoulders to rock and roll in leather zip trousers & stripey t-shirt of one heel what a picture. I am still in bed because my body craves rest and though its like a grave resting here so idly I cannot fathom New York or the world until the knot loosens further. I dont suppose [illegible] wanna read through another Hancock script. 'There's gonna be a Showdown' plays again.

A drawing of Doherty given to him by a

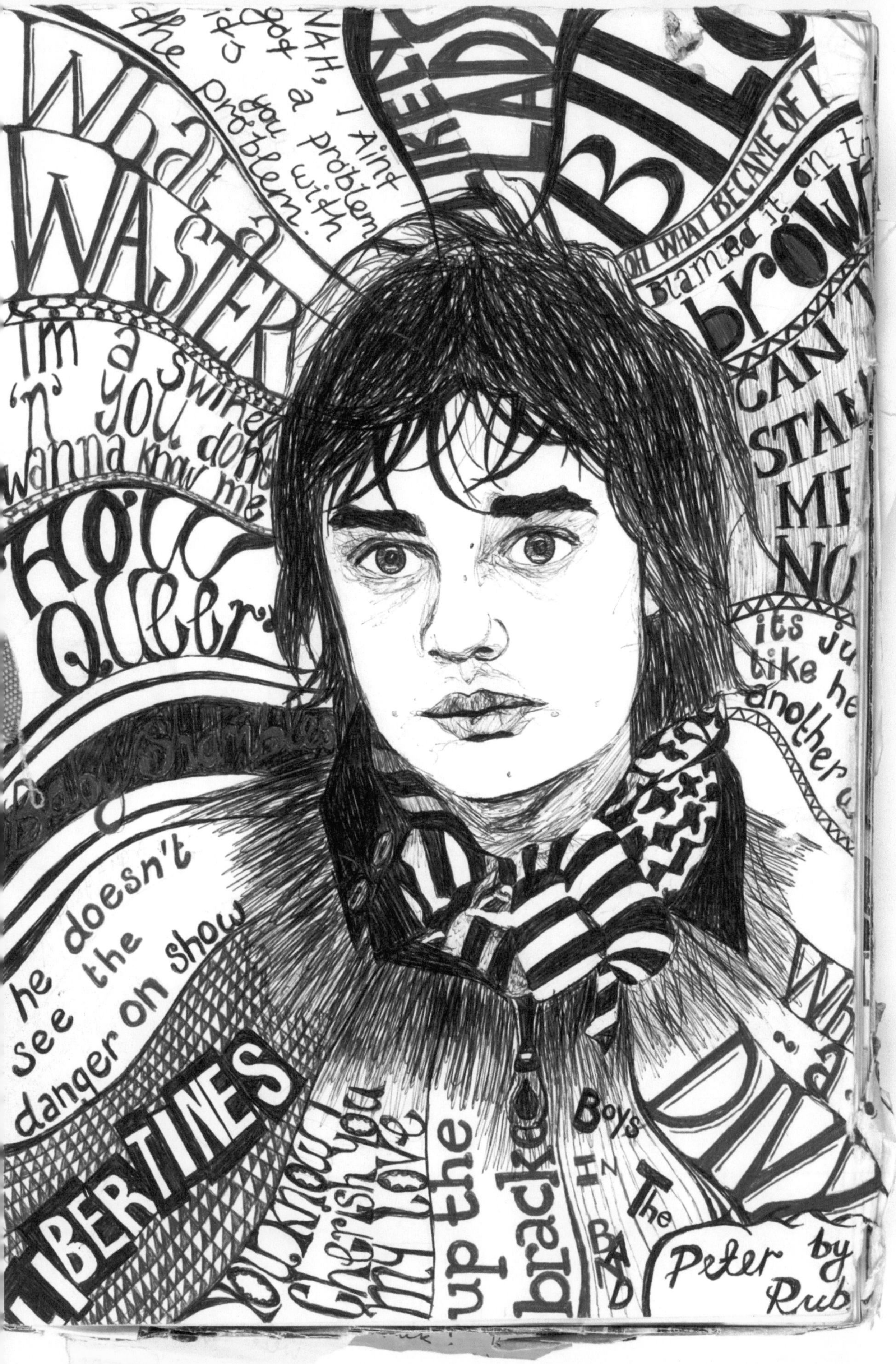
What a WASTER
NAH, I Aint got a problem with you
it's the problem.
OH WHAT BECAME OF
Blamed it on
I'm a swine 'n' you don't wanna know me
CAN
STAN
ME
NO
its ju
like he
another
he doesn't see the danger on show
Baby Shambles
BERTINES
cherish you
my love
up the
bracket
Boys
In
The
BAD
Peter by
Rub

The Observer
MUSIC
MONTHLY
OCTOBER 2005 NO 26
WORLD
EXCLUSIVE
PETE
DOHERTY'S
DIARIES
Plus sensational

A COLLAGE FROM DOHERTY'S DIARY
WITH MOUSTACHE BY KATE MOSS.
RAPHS BY JAMIE-JAMES MEDINA
fucked AGAIN.
CHOP OF PO
CHOP OF PO
KISS IS IT: Pete Doherty

my ... low.
I'm wherever you see ...
Your must be hearing those voices
again my son
"schizophrenic
your dad can see
you hate your friends
you burn your family
I dont know why you do
these things that you do"
special effects all mirrors
f special effects

The first cut was the deepest
long lost nights sobriety and
charity to the warmer feelings
war merits long lasting love and
deviance.

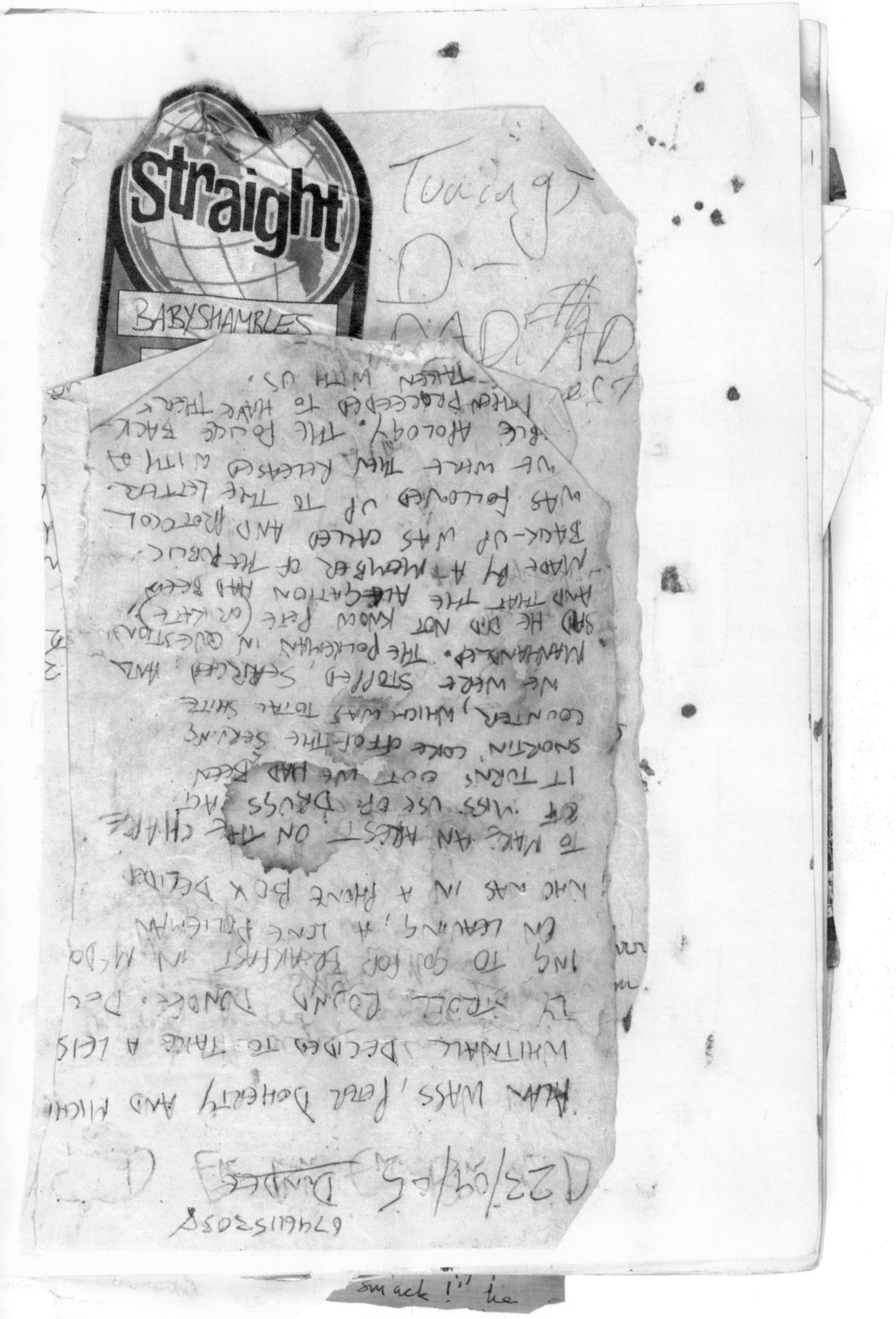
23/09/05 DUNDEE
67461153058
ALAN WASS, PETER DOHERTY AND MICH
WHITNALL DECIDED TO TAKE A LEIS
LY STROLL ROUND DUNDEE. DEC
ING TO GO FOR BREAKFAST IN McDO
ON LEAVING, A LONE POLICEMAN
WHO WAS IN A PHONE BOX DECIDED
TO MAKE AN AREST ON THE CHARGE
OF MISS USE OF DRUGS ACT.
IT TURNS OUT WE HAD BEEN
SNORTIN' COKE OFF OF THE SERVING
COUNTER, WHICH WAS TOTAL SHITE.
WE WERE STOPPED, SEARCHED AND
MANHANDLED. THE POLICEMAN IN QUESTION
SAID HE DID NOT KNOW PETE (OR KATE),
AND THAT THE ALLEGATION HAD BEEN
MADE BY A MEMBER OF THE PUBLIC.
BACK-UP WAS CALLED AND PROTOCOL
WAS FOLLOWED UP TO THE LETTER.
WE WERE THEN RELEASED WITH A
...BLE APOLOGY. THE POLICE BACK-
THEN PROCEEDED TO HAVE THEIR
TAKEN WITH US.

'Pipedown tour'
Alternative suggestions
'Carry on Scraping' tour 'Albion
'Dark side of the Spoon tour'
shambles or the whole sink the
last few weeks as a description
'Pipedown' is not quite apt
indeed Adam had 'Pipe up'
emblazoned across his bass drum
& Pat spent his ~~earnings~~ in advance ooh
3 days in & not on a

replacement for the guitar that
Islington Police still have under
lock & key. Along with my
suit from the time before (the time
before before), infernal ploddle
& this endless persecution.
free me, as one might print
on a £13 ~~T~~ T-shirt or was it £15?
Either way I miss Ann and Babs
took a fair few quid as Merch. Merch

2

Up ~~the morning~~

~~Fuck Forever~~

A ~~rebours~~

~~The 32nd of December~~

Pip~~edown~~

Dundee 23rd September 2005

The big old Jock bouncer gave it a good go up the nearplant. Another little fella popped out and so the puss ridden saga of my infected waist band regional danger zone continues. Anyway, here's Stu with a quick reminder .....

Fortune Favours

THE Brave

&

... en you Dead

... Snakes you have

Become one !

... s go where were wanted

... meet you at the cemetary

... Keats & Yeats are on

... side of Rubbie Burns

4

5

6

smack !" he

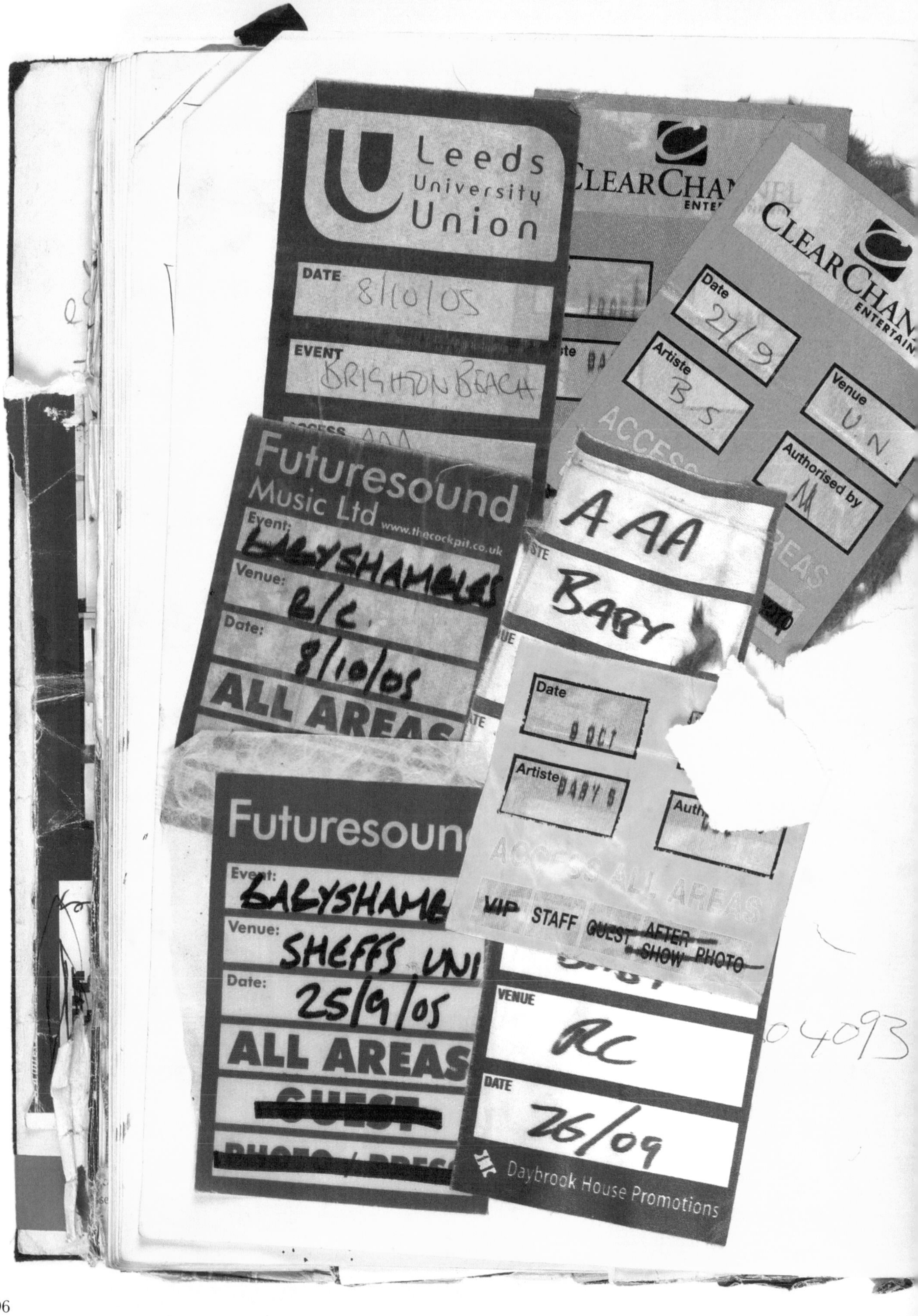
Leeds University Union
DATE 8/10/05
EVENT BRIGHTON BEACH
ClearChannel
Date 27/9
Artiste B S
Venue U N
Authorised by
Futuresound Music Ltd www.thecockpit.co.uk
Event: BABYSHAMBLES
Venue: B/C
Date: 8/10/05
ALL AREAS
AAA
BABY
Date 9 OCT
Artiste BABY S
ACCESS ALL AREAS
VIP STAFF GUEST AFTER SHOW PHOTO
Futuresound
Event: BABYSHAMB
Venue: SHEFFS UNI
Date: 25/9/05
ALL AREAS
VENUE RC
DATE 26/09
Daybrook House Promotions

and we slept-walked, sauntered and slid
and snuck across & allover Albion, Scotland
& Wales like good'uns. From the mentally
disabling opener at Carlisle to the confusion
& celebration of Brixton six hours sleep ago
we played mostly lengthy sets to a
run of sell-out shows, and mostly
enthusiastic fanz. Liverpool comes to
mind as the best one & there's a scramble at
the finishing post in the race for worst /
most fucked up gigle.

Even the old Bill mugging me off and
banging me up in Shrewsbury cannot offset
or tarnish the grand memories of that night.
Actually being on stage and not wanting
to run off into the nearest forest of
live deep underground has become
a more familiar feeling. Perhaps we are
getting there yet, Mr Doherty
Aside from all of which the tour
is the last of the gigs I
shall ever do in the shackles
of Babyshambles' relationship
with Matt 'Stokes Mr Burns'
Bates.

smack!' he

Peter Doherty

Up the Rs – my Hoops dreams

Last week Michael Nyman wrote in G2 about his plans for a fanfare for Queens Park Rangers, the football team he supports. But the Babyshambles singer believes the composer should step aside.

Fair play to Michael Nyman for composing the song for Queens Park Rangers to come out on to the pitch but I've already written a song for when they win the FA Cup. He could do the B-side.

Imagine a relationship that went wrong but you held on in there for years: that's what it is like supporting a football team. Your loyalty to a team can never die. Ties are stronger than they could ever be with a woman. If she goes and sleeps with your best mate, it's over. If the Rs' boss, Ian Holloway, slept with my best mate, QPR would still be my team. Even if many of the things that you loved about going to matches have gone – terraces, team shirts without sponsors and being able to smoke at grounds – you still stick with your team.

When I was a boy, I couldn't imagine anything other than going and living in Ellerslie Road or on the White City estate, near Loftus Road, where Rangers play. That's how central to my existence QPR was. I used to write a QPR fanzine, All Quiet on the Western Avenue. I was brought up in lots of different places, so there was a rootlessness to my life and the team gave me an identity. Playing football brought people together – we'd play against any brick wall, on any kerb, or see if we could put the window through in the art department.

My fondest memories involve things that happened off the pitch. I would climb into Loftus Road in the summer when the stadium was empty and sit there with my little book and pen, smoking a spliff behind the goal. One time, my girlfriend and I got into the dressing room and I stole a pair of shorts. That was one of the most romantic days of my life – snogging in the dressing room at QPR.

My song is a ska number. It goes like this: I'll be, I'll be there/And just before I hit the bar/With the ghost of Rodney Marsh in his pre-smug pundit days/Before he sold Rangers down the Swanee/With Gerry Francis's offshore money/It's a toss-up between Mick Jones/And a consortium from the Middle Eastern equivalent of Barrett Homes /I'll be, I'll be there/With blue and white ticker tape in my hair/Up the Rs/Up the Rs/Up the Rs/What a life on Mars.

I'm quite disappointed that I wasn't asked to write the QPR anthem. I'm doing my best for them. I've got a picture of the missus [Kate Moss] in the Rangers shirt inside the sleeve of the new Babyshambles album, Down in Albion. Now that is fantasy football ●

Peter Doherty is the lead singer of Babyshambles.

Tiff Needell

The car that's invisible to the naked eye

The w[...]
car is upon us. And it is [...]
cento. Scientists at Ri[...]
Houston, Texas, have [...]
made out of a single mole[...]
despite its size, has a cha[...]
and four wheels. Not a hug[...]
tion but worth a test drive n[...]

It has been eight years i[...]
ment (about twice as long [...]
Benz's latest technologica[...]
force, the S class) and is th[...]
in science's quest to con[...]
at an atomic level. The [...]
you see, is to have a ve[...]
something even the Tr[...]
manage – moving at[...]

Unsurprisingly, th[...]
approach the nan[...]
by its size. Or ra[...]
you can't see[...]
powerful ma[...]
nanometres a[...]
backs and bene[...]
that no matter [...]
the seat back, [...]
cramped. The [...]
no problem: yo[...]
nanocars side b[...]
human hair. A[...]
back to find a s[...]
between yours [...]

I'm told there [...]
"cars" made by [...]
this one has a dis[...]
the competition[...]
roll, rather than s[...]
60 atoms of carbo[...]
like a football – "[...]
frankly their road[...]
In fact, at room te[...]
road-holding [...]

waking up unable to breathe in a dark dusty bunk on a pitch black bus (the driver refusing to ~~was~~ waste energy) where is everyone? where am I? Any drugs about? is the chemical khazi still blocked?

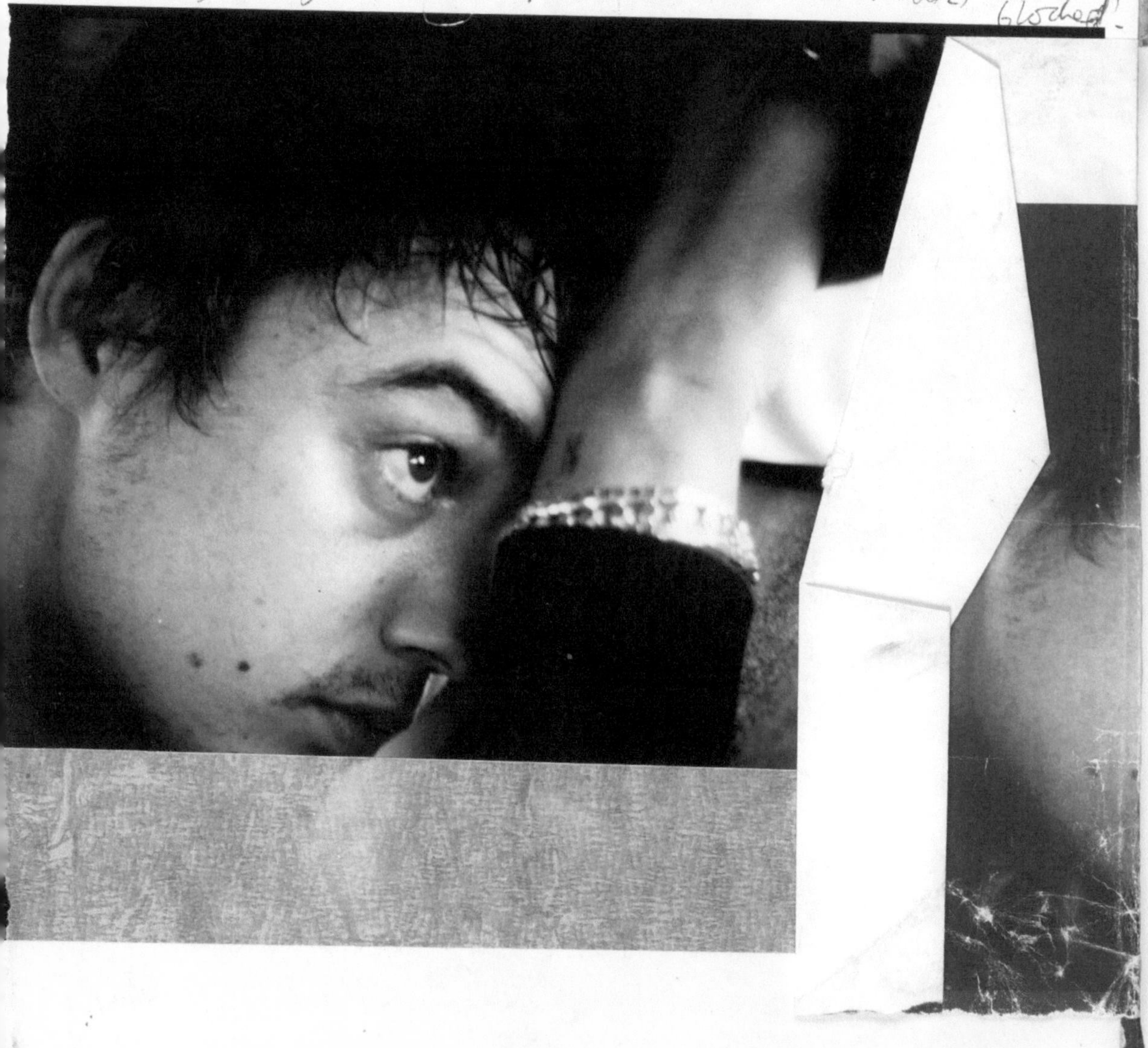

The bus had its moments of ~~[illegible]~~ claustrophobia & extreme paranoia .... but also a sense of togetherness was evident across the tour-map ... from town to town, forgetting the entourage & everyone else, the band was a band, intent on playing as a band and delighted only when crowds kicked off and truly embraced us

... smack!" he

a gottle
of
2B or not 2B

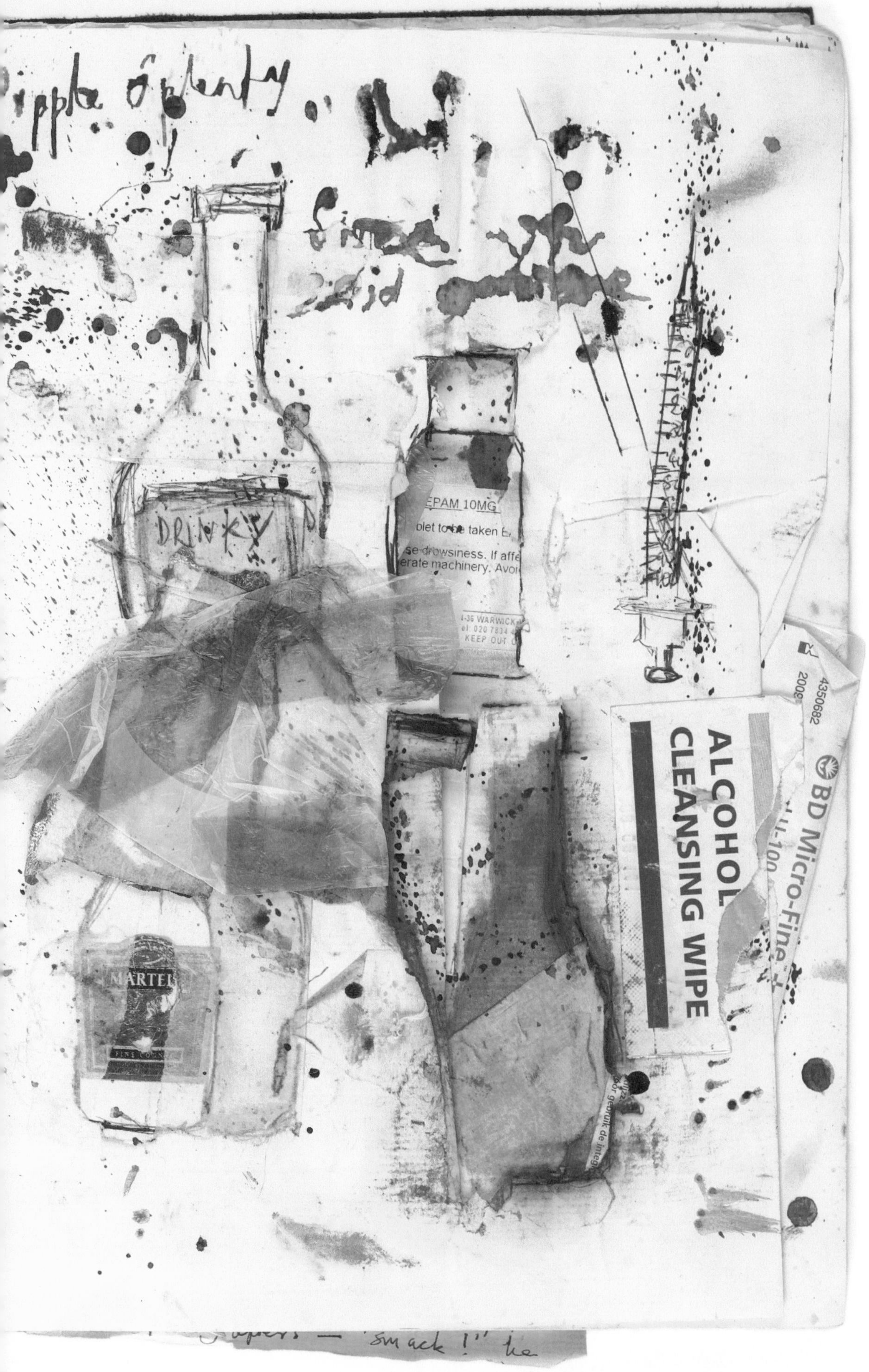
DRINK
EPAM 10MG
ALCOHOL
CLEANSING WIPE
BD Micro-Fine
4350682
MARTEL

The old gaseous kiss
now I've got a good gauze
smoker out the kiss
and then I load yours

washing-up bliss & the
morning finds me again
despite my foil-proof fool-free
plan,

Bones rattle all over the
minesweeping show. I am
advised to put some clothes
on and return to bed or
one or the other

uh oh A door takes the brunt
of someones pyschosis & not mine

A different Peter a darker
lighter Peter.

The sky is sky, hiding behind
the curtain ignoring me when I
ask the time.

The rotten void in my chest the has nestled oblivious but really is all but gone in terms of true terror. 10 vals a day & you know what else though does leave me a little shaken & withdrawn. Tucked up in bed with 9 mini martells, scrapey assortments instruments of musical torture. The walls are covered in indecipherable poetry sprayed on in blood.

unemployable – (a liability.
unworkable !

1. Insane
2. Dangerous
3. without the necessary conduct for someone in a 'job'ble situation, ie punctuality, sobriety, qualifications, experience, skills, knowledge, intelligence, health (see schedule

Questionable fella enough police work
to crap up your life's wall, drape
all the runs of blood and gum
smug mugs mush whack crack
the freaky shit they say about me
seekin' solace in the purity within
me
My country's my country make a
cunt or hero outa me.
Worse than a bout of bashing off
of a billion butch bruisers
is a look in your eyes that refuse
to let up
to let me suffer not when I'm not
locked up anyway I cocked up
your style a bit darling girl
and ruined all the whitest sheets
pissed in your bottles &
yeah got a Glasgow throttle
for a backhander in the snug
For single mothers everywhere in
love with crackheads you are
a shining light of hope.

Poor me poor me
poor me pour me another drink

days again in arcady. I have
been reunited with my love and
now the sun shines in Little
Farringdon. I'm in garden in
a towel & Kate is making
me a sandwich. There
are lilies in the pond &
my things & have been
out all night.
I have been knocked over by a
bus as I keep informing
everyone. My few weeks of
numbness, rage, derangement &
solitude were not part of a
design but my very core's
emptiest expression. Done for,
but my love has saved me
she's incredible you know....
aye let me explain.... —

car can never mind the fan belt
what about a belt for my dressing
gown. I'm having to make do with a
Dior tie. And the fans? Hanging
on in prayer, invisible speculation
I'm hanging on for the next
wave, Wolfie reaches for the joint
Nicotine fingers coiled to grasp
the purple smile. Gemma's eating
chopsticks, she may be nuts but
she's careful — she knows I took
it from the tele.

There's one small piece of good
news, charges have been dropped
we have to go back to the
tomb

Herbie rides again

Implant dont block rock just
brownstone so thats an opiate
free year a'coming up the woo
and you my love is who
I am doing it for all of a
sudden a man of my word.

yellowing classics
cannons at dawn
[coffee wallahs
pith helmets]
and 'an English son'?
Reebok classics
cannons at dawn
(terrible warlords
good warlords)
& an English song

Down in Albion
they're black & blue
but we dont talk about
that
are you from round he[re]
how do you do?
i'd like to talk about that
talk over ... Gin in teacups
leaves on the lawn
violence at bus stop[s]
& a pale thin girl with
eyes forlor[n]
Gin in teacups...
leaves on the lawn
violence in dole queues
& a pale thin girl boombacl[k]
behind the checkout
but if you're looking for a
cheap sort see in
False anticipation

Nothing I'd rather pummell
than the smug face of
a freelance tabloid
photographer

you have 25 minutes to live
turn the other cheek

remember a cramped cabin of stowaways
p the M1 lost in theories & opinion
omes I escorted all onto a
haos of Arcadys & pusses
omehow slumped the summer
nd the sun set without me
et am I broken?
Aye forlorn lost boy
a man from time to time
lemonade ride

might go out
or then may some
melancholic verse ~~[illegible]~~
rage across the lost pages

this book'll be lost soon
following my soul to
oblivion

the pen clangs
against vodka glass
green lime soda chimes
bring out your dead

I lay upon my spine-cracked bed
lost high upon the numbness
London sirens spin me to
sleep
& my rattling chest lunges at
breath

I wait for you my lov

X

miss you miss Moss the most
the clink of ice & the sound of
the radio. I'm all fucked up & sure
now but what of the meaning
to subscribe to this ribbon post
stone I'm at a crushing taken
all endeavour furrow & fervour
and further into the w

At who was it directed check in. He said
I was a mess. well done, Sherlock.
A fella gets knocked over by a
bus. Sweat dripping on a a
dead cigarette's blood. Advertisemen
Talk about me I'm silent & morose
what can I do for you? A drink
perhaps to wet the whistle?
Morning vomits up the daily routine
of despair & awkward delusion.
Temper temper Mollord.... kicking
off and trashing the joint.
I hosted a fortnight of freaked
out days.
I reside in pandemonium's parlour
half-lit, half-dead,

deepest
30th October 2005
whitechapel morning runs like
flood Annette throws keys
out an' that, some guard
but nonsense
phones abound like
something or other at
first sight 'just off Brick
Lane'

Metropolitan Police Service
MARTELL
FINE COGNAC

Anthony Aloysius St John Hancock *Radio T*

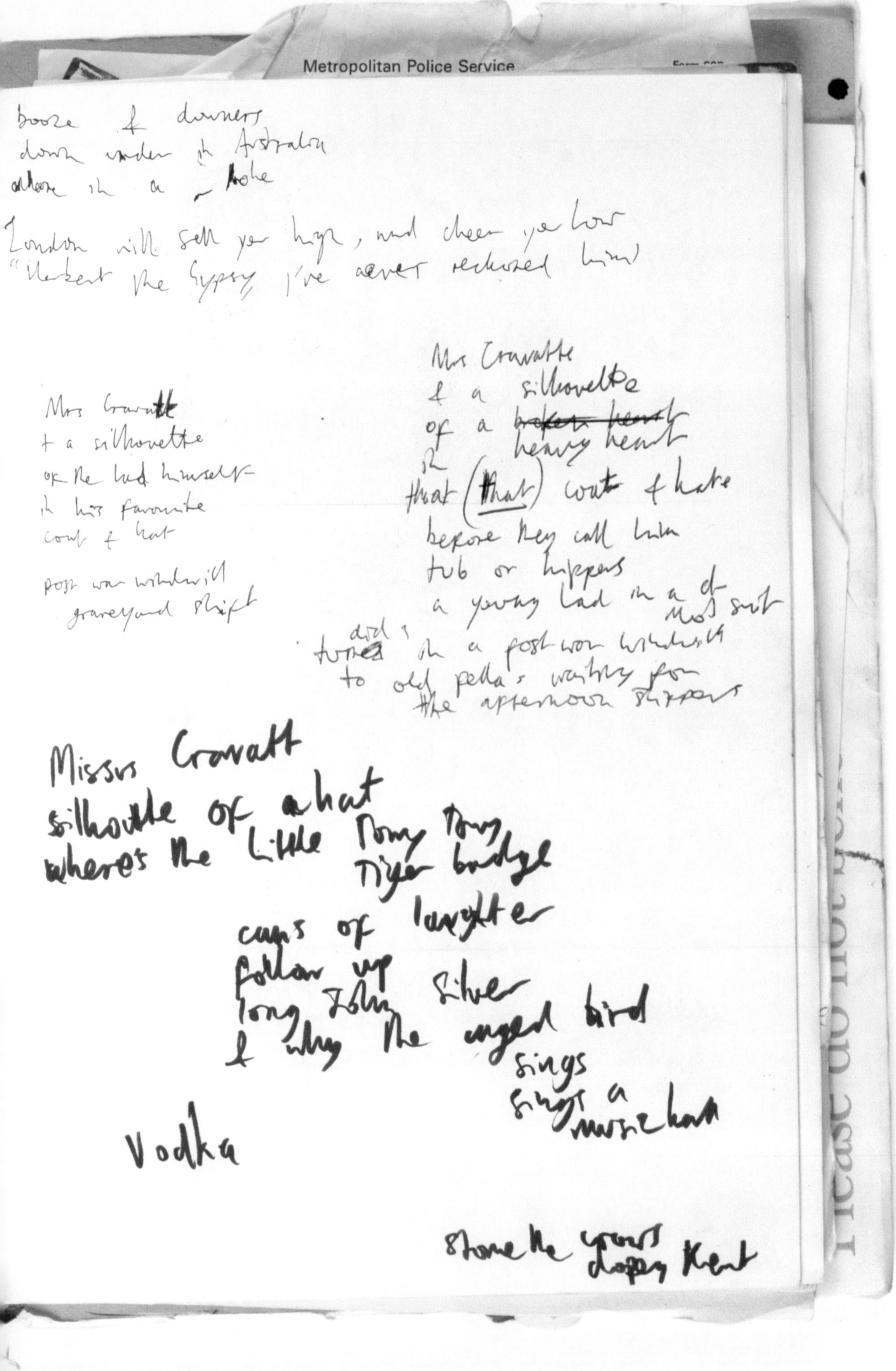
Metropolitan Police Service

booze & downers
down under in Australia
where in a ~ hole

London will sell you high, and cheer you low
"Herbert the Gypsy I've never reckoned him"

Mrs Cravatt
& a silhouette
of the lad himself
in his favourite
coat & hat

post war windmill
graveyard shift

Mrs Cravatte
& a silhouette
of a ~~broken heart~~
heavy heart
in
that (that) coat & hat
before they call him
tub or kippers
a young lad in a demob suit
~~turned~~ and in a post war windmill
to old fella's waiting for
the afternoon strippers

Missus Cravatt
silhouette of a hat
where's the little Tony Tony
Tiger badge
cups of laughter
follow up
long John Silver
& why the caged bird
sings
sings a
music hall

Vodka

Stone the crows
droopy Kent

and clearly the colours
sharply cut half cut
thoughts came out blanker
than the colours, emptier
than my heart. O, goddess
features & diabolical writings.
do this or that well &
save your reputation
from 'Darling crackhead'
to little beauty I take
the next year off.....

Metropolitan Police Service

Form ...

~~A~~ She knows my heart &
Soul are ~~coloured~~ this
rattling so...

now
she ~~the~~ disconnects from
all that I am, a filthy ~~mitt~~ measure
of long lost devotion — barely a
drop in her ocean. I mean to tell her

not to ~~let~~ to

I want to kiss her mostly ~~al~~
& then say it again

Her face teases men like lust or spinning
barrels of Russian roulette. One kiss
leaves me worthless — worth less than
a self satisfied smirk — which she
has mastered. Another kiss leaves me

breathless (although she will doubt that
with precision in gesture: and this the
final working nail in the coffin of
some ancient belief I can't tell you
~~so~~ now because she's reading over
my shoulder even as I scribble untidily
away in the stall we say no mans land
of ~~L~~ Lakeyet and fuck off

or turn over ...

Please do not ...

Metropolitan Police Service Form 60B

I'm not supposed to wonder what I did wrong, the simplicity & clinical finality of their judgements.... their 'charges' as I charge about the country and my mind bucking & bronking through the wastelands of the ether the ravaged lands that I continue to prowl, for the lift the drift & the fall. Basking in the grandest generous displays of hero worship that generally accompany's my every staged show of shambles.

What I did wrong was to write & sing immense songs & continue to live a wastrels squalid life

Up & down & inside out
with flesh or mind fled youth about
your decay to blind the sight of shout
of pouts the ~~krally~~ roaring mouth

To whom it may concern,

Recent high pressive buildup
of drug charges to deliberately cobbled together cases for the prosecution,
taking its toll heart & soul
when not only the dice dont roll
in your favour & the only reality
to savour is another cobbled together view

"D'you know what I mean"
Viva le Wolfe

…aise the Kaboose

…ight it just my luck? Its said that to write in
…ed is all [illegible] bad luck upon the writers head...
and oh no. fuck, every night I've been writing
in blood red blood and now the luck is all in
…ight again: ~~could~~ it be with the lighter dim.....

Scarlet, vermillion, Rouge or Cherry Ripe

The pied piper of tower hamlets licks
~~[illegible]~~ the pipe & well he might......

Soon all pressing matters have no concern
~~[illegible]~~

[unto Arcady ~~[illegible]~~ with a tickle town
first class open return

raise the roof
& raise & blaze the kaboose, belt out a tune
my bloody words will lead me to doom
as writing in red brings misfortune

Pete the poet

JESSICA SMITH discovers a polite and sensitive side to Pete Doherty in an EXCLUSIVE interview with the junkie rock star

"I'm part of celebrity culture but I'm also part of a hospital waiting list"

BEFORE he was famous, Babyshambles frontman Pete Doherty worked as a paper-boy for the *East London Advertiser.*

When I met him on Saturday night at the Premises studio on Hackney Road, Bethnal Green, I told him I'd been nervous about coming after hearing reports he'd punched a *Radio One* reporter in the arm.

But he said: "I'd never hit an *Advertiser* reporter. I like the paper, I read it all the time. I even used to deliver it."

When I was invited to meet the 27-year-old rock star, I expected a snatched two-minute interview before he rushed off to some glamorous party.

But I ended up spending most of Saturday night with the thoroughly polite and friendly Babyshambles.

I waited for Doherty, who lives in Laburnum Street in the caf next door to the studio.

Looking nervous and tired, he came to collect me in person, greeting me politely with a handshake and a peck on the cheek.

I followed him into the studio, where he told me, stumbling: "I'm not really giving interviews at the moment. The nationals only care about the drugs."

In the studio, which featured a small stage, carpets on the walls, and a battered sofa, I was treated to a free Babyshambles concert.

As a band, they are tight, inventive, and focussed; only stopping for one beer break during a two-hour recording session.

When they finished playing, Doherty led me to a staircase in a back corridor of the studio, where he lit the first of many cigarettes, and talked to me distractedly, but openly. I asked him how he was doing. Thoughtfully, he said: "We have these little apocalypses."

The softly-spoken musician looked uncomfortable discussing his high-profile relationship with supermodel Kate Moss. After a series of bust-ups, the pair are now rumoured to be planning a summer wedding.

He admitted: "She had a go at me, saying that I love the drama. I shouldn't talk about it. But in spite of all the legal stuff, life is going well."

Doherty has lived in East London since dropping out of university to pursue musical fame.

Despite his rock and roll media image, the musician describes himself as 'bookish'.

After growing up in army barracks, he scored top marks at GCSE and 'A' level, and won a national poetry competition when he was just 16.

He said: "At 13, I was reading Orwell – *1984*, and *Down and Out in Paris and London*.

"Then I read poets: Suskind, Dickinson, and later on Verlaine and Baudelaire – his essays on wine and hashish, and his stuff on women and on prostitutes is very interesting."

He worked at East Side Books on Brick Lane before his former band, the Libertines, hit the big time, and these days visits Spitalfields market to find new titles.

"Music has never been number one,' he told me. "I'm mostly into words and hats."

When I asked him if he'd ever thought about being a novelist, his eyes lit up for the first time during our 45-minute conversation.

"Every day I think about it," he said. "Writing and music thrive off each other, they goad each other along, they make something complete."

Doherty formed the Libertines with Carl Barat after they met as students. The band became known for performing 'guerilla gigs', sometimes at Doherty and Barat's own flat on Bethnal Green Road.

Their self-titled second album reached number one in the music charts, but Doherty left the band after a falling-out over his drug use.

He then formed Babyshambles, and in January 2005 met Moss at her 30th birthday party. But when Moss was photographed snorting cocaine at a studio where Babyshambles were rehearsing, he was accused of being a bad influence on the 32-year-old mother-of-one, who lost multi-million pound contracts over the scandal.

He told me: "A lot of these things, I block them out."

Although he confessed that the implant he had fitted to beat his heroin addiction is not a 'quick fix', he says is getting better: "Rehab is the best thing that could happen to me, and I'm glad I wasn't let off the hook completely."

Pete Doherty rehearses with his band Babyshambles on Hackney Road. RIGHT: a cop car lurks outside Pete's East End flat

As well as music and literature, Doherty is also committed to politics. He is passionately anti-war.

"Iraq is not even a war," he said, "it's an unholy mess. The cost, the lives, the endless use of resources – it's just a matter of time before it causes a wave of tsunami proportions."

But he is excited by East End politics, saying: "East London has always been a haven for radicals. And people like Respect are fighting for a lot of things I believe in. I am a socialist.

"But I think I missed out on the George Galloway funfair. I believe in community, I am not so much into personalities."

So I asked him if he ever wished he could go back to being a normal person.

"But I am a normal person!" he exclaimed, adding: "You can't touch fame, it doesn't really exist outside you and the money. It's a funny old game.

"I am part of celebrity culture, but I am also part of a hospital waiting list.

"And to the people who are worried about me being a bad role model for young people – why do media only focus on the drugs then?"

Here's looking forward to the novel.

Babyshambles play the Love Music Hate Racism festival in Trafalgar Square, central London, on Saturday.

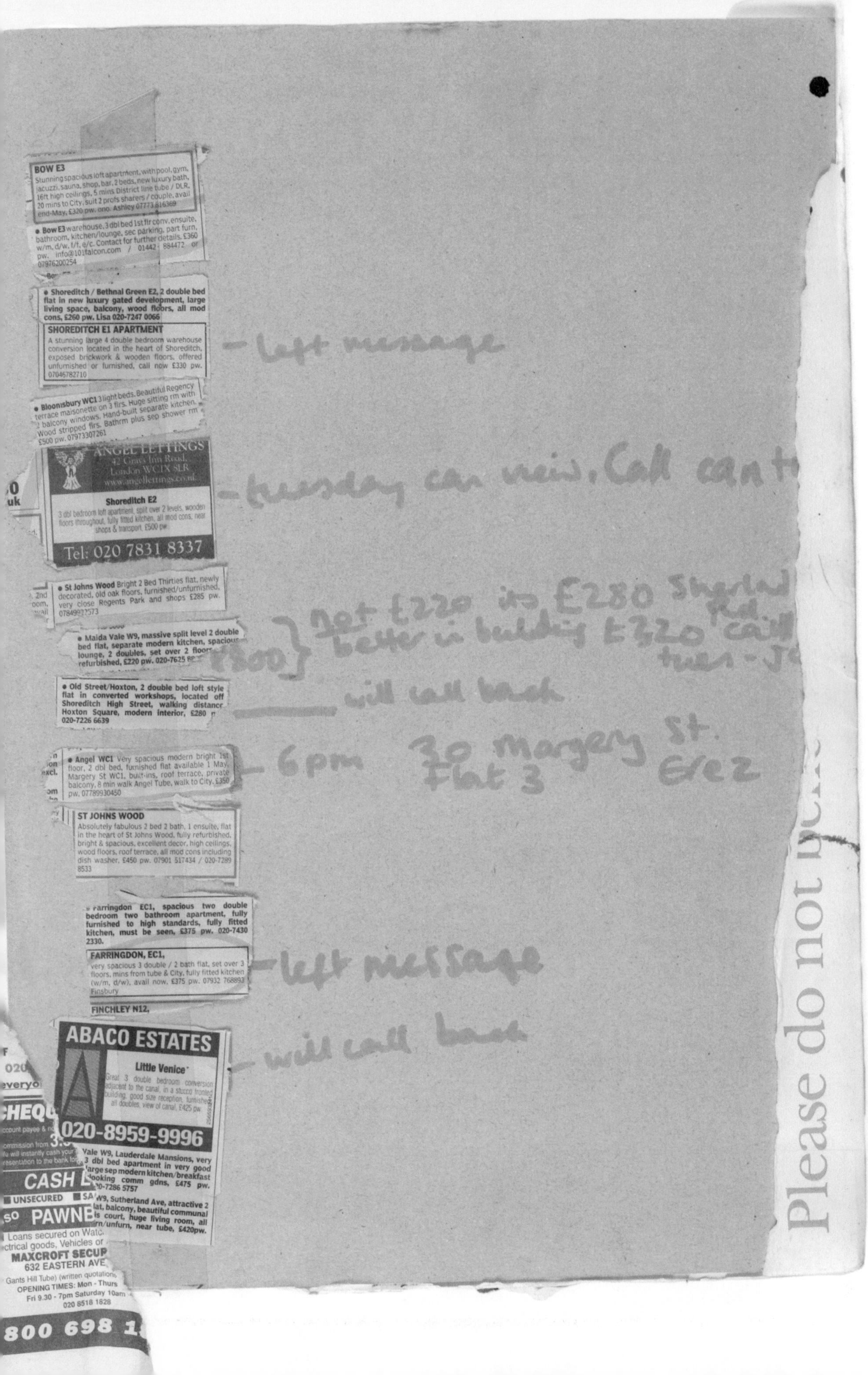
BOW E3
Stunning spacious loft apartment, with pool, gym, jacuzzi, sauna, shop, bar, 2 beds, new luxury bath, 16ft high ceilings, 5 mins District line tube / DLR, 20 mins to City, suit 2 profs sharers / couple, avail end-May, £320 pw. ono. Ashley 07773 816369
• Bow E3 warehouse, 3 dbl bed 1st flr conv, ensuite, bathroom, kitchen/lounge, sec parking, part furn, w/m, d/w, f/f, c/c. Contact for further details. £360 pw. info@101falcon.com / 01442 884472 or 07976200254
• Shoreditch / Bethnal Green E2, 2 double bed flat in new luxury gated development, large living space, balcony, wood floors, all mod cons, £260 pw. Lisa 020-7247 0066
SHOREDITCH E1 APARTMENT
A stunning large 4 double bedroom warehouse conversion located in the heart of Shoreditch, exposed brickwork & wooden floors, offered unfurnished or furnished, call now £330 pw. 07046782710
– left message
• Bloomsbury WC1 3 light beds. Beautiful Regency terrace maisonette on 3 flrs. Huge sitting rm with 2 balcony windows. Hand-built separate kitchen. Wood stripped flrs. Bathrm plus sep shower rm £500 pw. 07973307261
ANGEL LETTINGS
42 Grays Inn Road, London WC1X 8LR
www.angellettings.co.uk
Shoreditch E2
3 dbl bedroom loft apartment, split over 2 levels, wooden floors throughout, fully fitted kitchen, all mod cons, near shops & transport. £500 pw
Tel: 020 7831 8337
– tuesday can view. Call can to
• St Johns Wood Bright 2 Bed Thirties flat, newly decorated, old oak floors, furnished/unfurnished, very close Regents Park and shops £285 pw. 07849972573
• Maida Vale W9, massive split level 2 double bed flat, separate modern kitchen, spacious lounge, 2 doubles, set over 2 floors refurbished, £220 pw. 020-7625
£800 } not £220 its £280 Sherland Rd. better in building £320 call tues - J
• Old Street/Hoxton, 2 double bed loft style flat in converted workshops, located off Shoreditch High Street, walking distance Hoxton Square, modern interior, £280 020-7226 6639
will call back
• Angel WC1 Very spacious modern bright 1st floor, 2 dbl bed, furnished flat available 1 May, Margery St WC1, built-ins, roof terrace, private balcony, 8 min walk Angel Tube, walk to City. £350 pw. 07789930450
6pm 30 Margery St. Flat 3 Erez
ST JOHNS WOOD
Absolutely fabulous 2 bed 2 bath, 1 ensuite, flat in the heart of St Johns Wood, fully refurbished, bright & spacious, excellent decor, high ceilings, wood floors, roof terrace, all mod cons including dish washer, £450 pw. 07901 517434 / 020-7289 8533
• Farringdon EC1, spacious two double bedroom two bathroom apartment, fully furnished to high standards, fully fitted kitchen, must be seen, £375 pw. 020-7430 2330.
FARRINGDON, EC1,
very spacious 3 double / 2 bath flat, set over 3 floors, mins from tube & City, fully fitted kitchen (w/m, d/w), avail now, £375 pw. 07932 768893 Finsbury
– left message
FINCHLEY N12,
ABACO ESTATES
Little Venice
Great 3 double bedroom conversion adjacent to the canal, in a stucco fronted building, good size reception, furnished, all doubles, view of canal, £425 pw.
020-8959-9996
– will call back
Vale W9, Lauderdale Mansions, very 3 dbl bed apartment in very good large sep modern kitchen/breakfast looking comm gdns, £475 pw. 020-7286 5757
W9, Sutherland Ave, attractive 2 flat, balcony, beautiful communal is court, huge living room, all furn/unfurn, near tube, £420pw.
CHEQU
CASH
UNSECURED
PAWNB
Loans secured on Watc
MAXCROFT SECUR
632 EASTERN AVE
OPENING TIMES: Mon - Thurs Fri 9.30 - 7pm Saturday 10am
020 8518 1828
800 698 1
Please do not bend

COME SLOWLY, EDEN!

24th Dec 2005

once twice A yeah upon
a time
Unbilotitled unnumbered journal
unsettled radroachive to pick Inselling familiar
readies out an Arm In another 10 years
none of us will be like that anymore after all
Absently minded made the mark on paper
Going straight through to London (Waterloo)
Manchester (Peterloo)
Glastonbury (Porterloo)

Anywhere in Albion. I am high above the Porter pub, a maze of staircased up rooms, my arm just about ready to fall off although I am loathe to dwell on my pen dwelling hours (like all the books seem to ... opening with some maple push with blood and promise of vows that shoot to shot the shit vows near the visions inside yourself ownerism of great peace. Funny about this and that thought ... radiant detention nodding off – akip'd & equipped for a sleep in ... everywhere looks so milky

I wore the willomon coat / let the gas or cocaine gloat
Missus Crowatt aghast / at the Aphrodite or the Watering Hole
no hidden cameras then, in long lost civilizations,
Libertines, nymphs, shades in pool side raves
then nights ravens; wolves & gloves from the job
through wars and film stories for war films

A fool there was
A fool there was
incision after incision
I spike myself because
if ever a fool there was
was a fool there was

but you can't put that on me
no you can't put that on me
I know what you say about me
+ I mostly agree
but you can't put that on me REPEAT

A fool there was
A fool there was
decision after decision
never learn from mistakes because
ever a fool there was
was a fool there was ....

and all your tastes + preferences
are measured out in Moscow miles
+ lo .. the wolf prints in the snow
that led us off the straight + narrow
crooked smiles that frown
I saw many sad goodbyes
longer say hello....

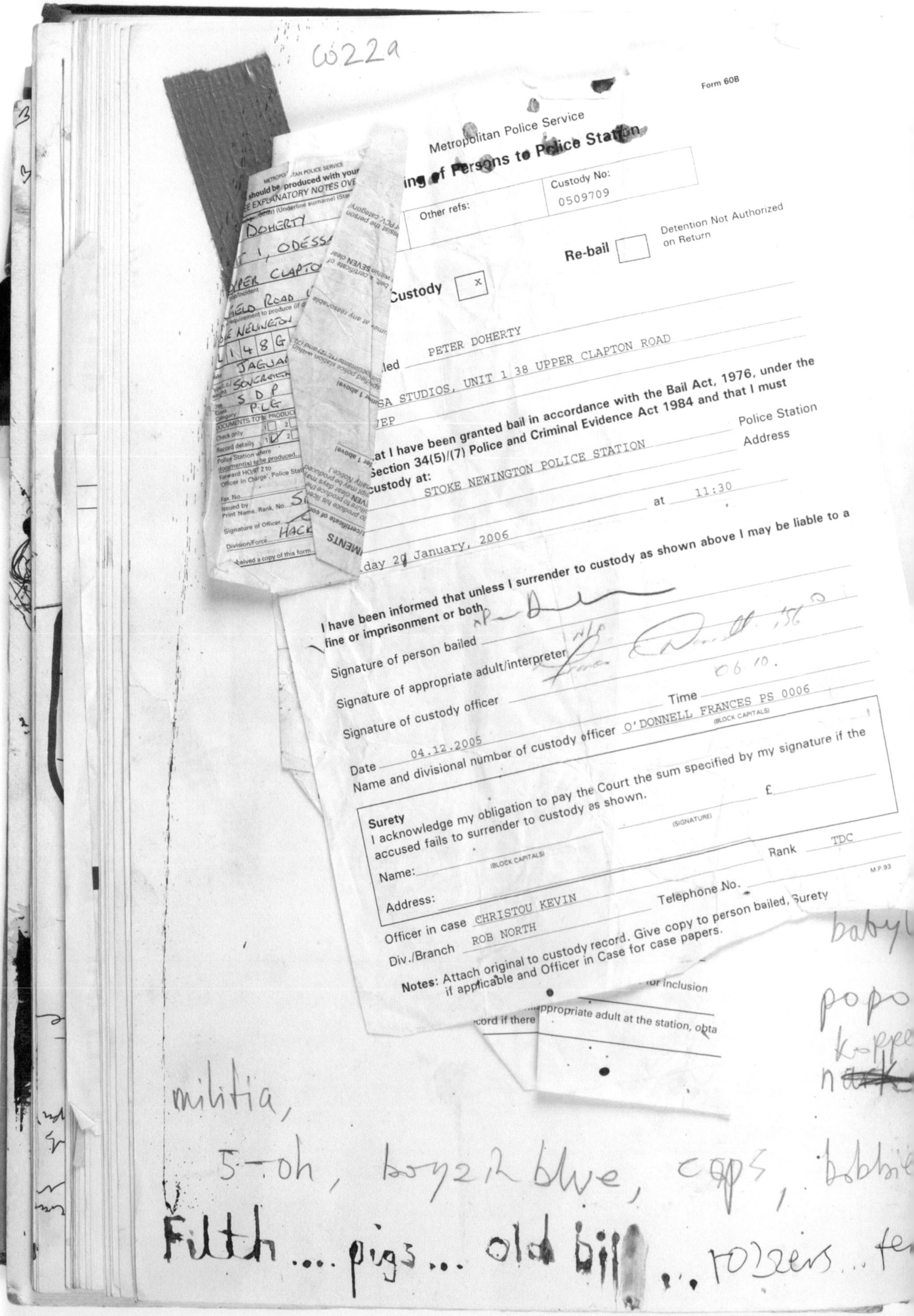

CO22a
Form 60B
Metropolitan Police Service
ing of Persons to Police Station
Custody No:
0509709
Other refs:
Re-bail
Detention Not Authorized on Return
Custody
X
led PETER DOHERTY
SA STUDIOS, UNIT 1 38 UPPER CLAPTON ROAD
at I have been granted bail in accordance with the Bail Act, 1976, under the Section 34(5)/(7) Police and Criminal Evidence Act 1984 and that I must custody at:
Police Station
Address
STOKE NEWINGTON POLICE STATION
at 11:30
day 20 January, 2006
I have been informed that unless I surrender to custody as shown above I may be liable to a fine or imprisonment or both
Signature of person bailed
Signature of appropriate adult/interpreter
Signature of custody officer
Time 06 10.
Date 04.12.2005
Name and divisional number of custody officer O'DONNELL FRANCES PS 0006
(BLOCK CAPITALS)
Surety
I acknowledge my obligation to pay the Court the sum specified by my signature if the accused fails to surrender to custody as shown.
£
(SIGNATURE)
Name:
(BLOCK CAPITALS)
Rank TDC
Address:
Telephone No.
M.P. 93
Officer in case CHRISTOU KEVIN
Div./Branch ROB NORTH
Notes: Attach original to custody record. Give copy to person bailed, Surety if applicable and Officer in Case for case papers.
METROPOLITAN POLICE SERVICE
should be produced with your
SEE EXPLANATORY NOTES OVER
DOHERTY
1, ODESSA
UPPER CLAPTON
ROAD
STOKE NEWINGTON
JAGUAR
SDP
PLG
DOCUMENTS TO BE PRODUCED
Check only
Record details
Police Station where document(s) to be produced
Forward HO/RT 2 to 'Officer in Charge', Police Station
Issued by Print Name, Rank, No.
Signature of Officer
Division/Force HACK
received a copy of this form
militia,
5-oh, boyz in blue, cops, bobbie
Filth.... pigs... old bill... rozzers...
baby
popo
koppe

London : here and there a deserving recipient of
my awe & gratitude in these more reflective & peaceful
moments in the maelstrom of ~~contemporary~~ Bilo's day
to day writing drugging singing & (receiving & otherwise) stinging
Somehow Laburnum Street remains Albion Rooms' host ; and
a traffic ~~that~~ deep pavement syrup was todays most common scenery-
set theme as Whitnall & I raced back & forth to Heathrow...
by mid afternoon General had given up the role of
good guy/ event coordinator and instead flared up, tossed
chairs across Golden Grove & cast Mick asunder.
Hours on from the exhausted Rasta's ferocious reaction to my
sudden independence, I am still aiming to keep all promises
and another comes hand in hand with narcotic tick + roll
lessons with Chi-chi in the form of our 3rd roadside
went-out with the boys in blue. Dagen Polise .....
the dragon police waiting by the gates
It's nothing, neither nappo less pi-rolous than the
continuing darkening voices that surround me
and in the current climate of constant~~ly~~ & chaotic
Thames Magistrate set-pieces it is just further jogs to
the memory : do not carry anything ; dickhead!
charges coming out of my arse
trumped up possessions & suspicion of drugging motor cars
that are already ours .....

another police station holiday for all of the
legal hours
cells the dustbins & us daft lot the flowers
but Bilo never before the law cowers
justice sleeps & ~~[illegible]~~ lashings of fuckery soups
the mix

The flat is cold enough now, the large main room
scattered with the remains of my material days
So much has gone - for a Burton I could probably
sue the actor's estate - hmmm.

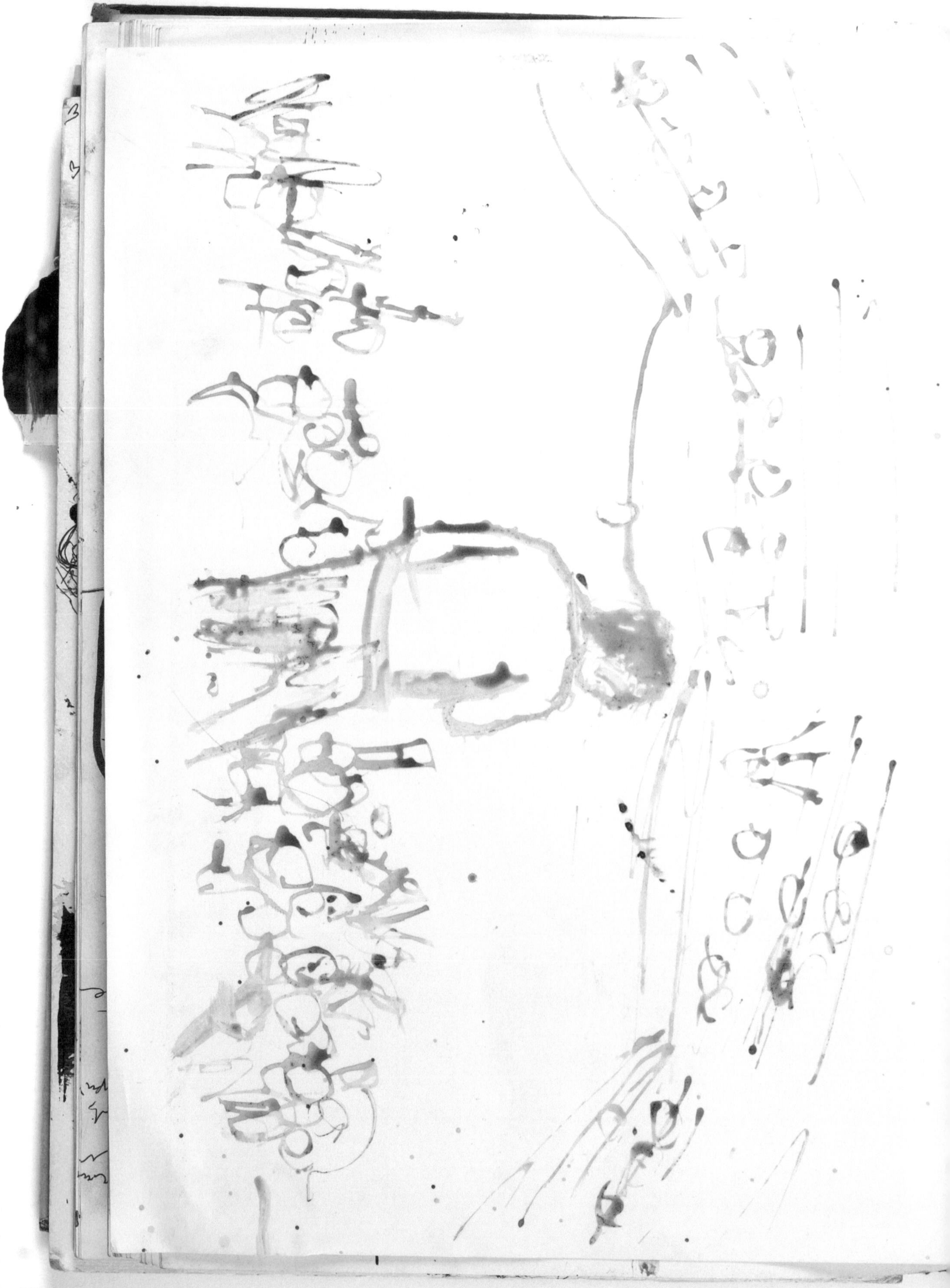

must I draw from it all the very nourishment for my moral life? whose morality denies me? For my own sake — because they have the power to cut off my head it feels like — I must become a hero, to organize my life & obtain from it what they deny me.
If I live in order to continue to live with myself I must have more talent than the most exquisite poet.
These people can only put up with the tamed heroes — they dont know about heroism

These things are sold before they really are lost forever. Pockets full of rocks on a murder scene, followed ~~Some mountain~~ trail with the close clan roads around the gaff (must've been the jag), threw most actually all over some netting by the chalk-like silhouettes jumping on and off the parade and into pop martydom mountains.
A chinese or Italian couple were dubious about my intentions in their ~~shop was it~~
Seems to me to be a chase for liberty — eplected in this my reality — chasing open backed buses and leaping on in search of ...... the bus I suppose.

Prior to that, under & over my blanket quota of blankies . . . . .

these words are born darkly fearfully afar . . . .
poetry is divine, the centre & circumference of all estrangement and collect

my words are loyal too loyal
to my life. They know about
the phantoms about me

How [illegible]
mean to be content.

been about melody .. but melody & I met in many depraved situations. Meeting melody is the victory of the empty, spiralling nightmare – Empty in the superficial sense

Its pretty weird really, being led all fucked up through the slite-pipe of the judicial system, clanging & a distant radio, Lashing out in anger – dont let the whistle stop, follow the silence into dreams

Still old son it aint all learning dark voices. Wont

for the tonight

let this be uncorrected proof of my
meagre existence waiting on key jangles
still and the roll of peeled oranges
to enjoy. Words still are timeless &
need no bail to impale the attention of
man so am I now no better off.
A junky they call me and I'll refuse nothing
yet (excepting a piss test, aha!)
Am I not a fantastic idiot
All good art comes from agony
not all great art comes from agony

LET THEM ~~EAT CAKE~~

The nurses in our prisons & rehabs are always massive & African.

She held up a load of skanky white bread slices: 'You want bread'

LET THEM SMOKE CRACK

'no do you have any cake?'

'wait . . .'

So I wait. And cake comes and an Orange too. Yoo-hoo. (note: spooky thing on tele)

So I said to the nurse as she came to the flap after years since I'd pressed the emergency buzzer 'I just had the strangest dream'

'Oh really'

'Yeah'

Pauses pauses

'I dreamt that you got me some tobacco and I gave you £50 —'

'You want tobacco? . . .'

LET THEM SMOKE BACCY

CARE THEM LET

Breaking into heaven that's what dreams are – so how about waking into hell with a thick heavy chest and snifple. Afore the living sickly me came the cousin of death who was ruining some gig for potential punters by miming along to the prime time BBC shite that played as I slept. I wont even tell you what it was as it will expose me and my journalkeeping as nonsense designed only to keep my hands warm as the song wasnt that unbefitting the dark mood of the dream which somehow carries upon a recent theme of making it at the 11th 12th or 13th hour to gigs and all manner of inconvenia-bilities occurring (such as me painting myself copper & miming I'm walking in the air, there, I said it now)

And thats not the point . . . . I awake sharply, dreamily into the cold reality of the prison. It is fucking cold anyway, whenever you read this, and it might be in some fit Richards like bath (you know the one I mean)

Not leniency, not luck,
not your love, nor your
loathing
only your law
I want to snatch it and
smash it and
snort it and
smoke it up
Apelikes into justice, brimful
of fag ash in sickly mornings
I dreamt of playing music,
one way or another. There
was a child also. Revolting
and centre of attention.
Long splashing flushing nights,
flushing naked (save the grey
thick socks) Someone sort me out
now I couldnae give a fuck
2 fucks
for the rest of the world watches
on only as I sit here useless
to 'em all

viva le French clogs

Monday 5th Feb

The day is bright in dartmoor but I feel rougher than a rough pair of shitty old boots until my methadone & that holds me awhile. Innit marvellous eh? I am the sick man of Europe after all and a prize turkey at that.

Cold " ——————— "

The path is murky Lord — and mock and scoff ye not future Libertine because I'm in it up to me neck just now and it aint looking Rosey gardens for the 8th d.t.o dip squads d.r.r. community drug orders and good old fashioned bird are the delectable choices on the palette of persecution ... prosecution, torsication. Not so eloquent this day our daily hardened slice of skanky white bread. Pray to goodness Young and old coz I need y'all to bail me out of this one.

Fuck martyrdom — where's me walk by the canal?

Ah man the memories. Racing up to sheppfeld in 203 jaguars for gigs where we blew apart the regime I'm talking about something fucking powerful all colours classes and cultures melting into a valve
Or them truly days sketching into Arcady, castle like country stone houses with churches in the chapel and true love over the ~~e~~ country orchard ~~of~~ flowers
Racing an old car across the open fields, ~~old~~ barns with amps & guitars & drumkits & stepping down secret staircases to burn ancient cushions in rages & fits of love & doped delerium
fixing up in the summer house surrounded by my ruins my beloved tiles & trinkets. Ignoring the world. Ah, she saw me happy for awhile there until rage and parallel universes collided.
Imagine somehow poison being proved not to exist in someones heart Imagine being unlocked from this cell.

You're free to go French dog
Well fuck

It took 3 strokes of the axe to take Mary's head off. The dog moved beneath her dismembered skirt - The executioner holding only her bloody wig
Fucking hell!! That'd be alright

Dear oh dear the tug o'war betwixt
Herr Dis Comfort & his unfathomably
discourteous (ex)wife ~~..~~ Stacy
Rallying towards the dirt track on a
sizzling dusty hot summers day

Beside the edge of the forest a figure
lay in a heap under plastic sheets
dead, but still sweating yellow puss in
the hot hot heat.

Mouthing anticipation now for the return
capers that once took themselves until paper
hats became sabres & goodmorning
small talk to neighbours : evidence for
the spill on the papers
Bets being taken on the repetition
of tunes & relating to this very room

Two or three hardly cause for the doors to
be permanently manned but still my
careless trust is set up perfectly - pathetically
(tower of cards) for another

da h oze

Manys the time
I made to go
to hit the road ... just a ~~cripple~~ cheats noise

Probation report, 21st February 2006

Dum speron spero – even if that
rattling cough is breath's only audible
refrain. Years of Shamblin' living and
intense & dedicated crack & smack
abuse have proven to be an obvious but
equally problematic/ introduction to the
[in retrospect] desired abstinence
that I must be
laying foundations
for in this the first
leg of the court order.

My heart and lips are somewhat numbed by
the push & pull-me of my heads rowdy
scheme & sentiment traffic flow & stutter, that
the once fulfilling & sustainable life of
~~that~~ that whimsy & luck & and pop
mythology & triumphantly & benignly reigned
over & upon.

Words often said to have had
some remarkable away ways over the
years & by my own experience I've learnt
~~to~~ of poetry's power in the realm of
the heart & the lips.

POETRY & GUITAR / WORDS slogans & GUNS

H.M.P.
PENTONVILLE

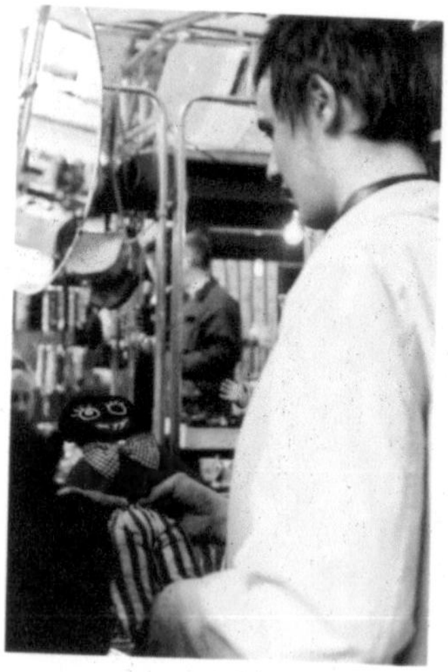

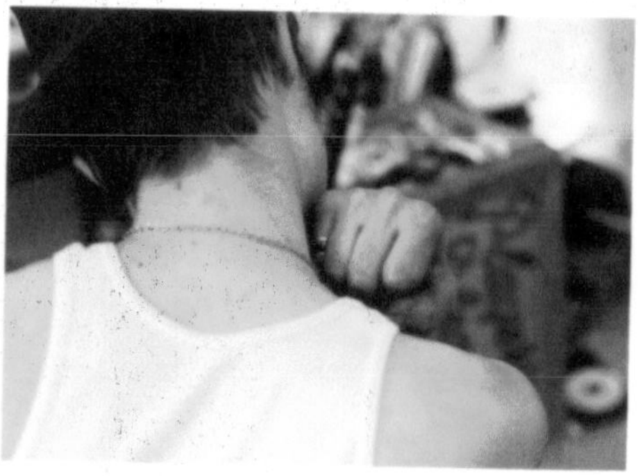

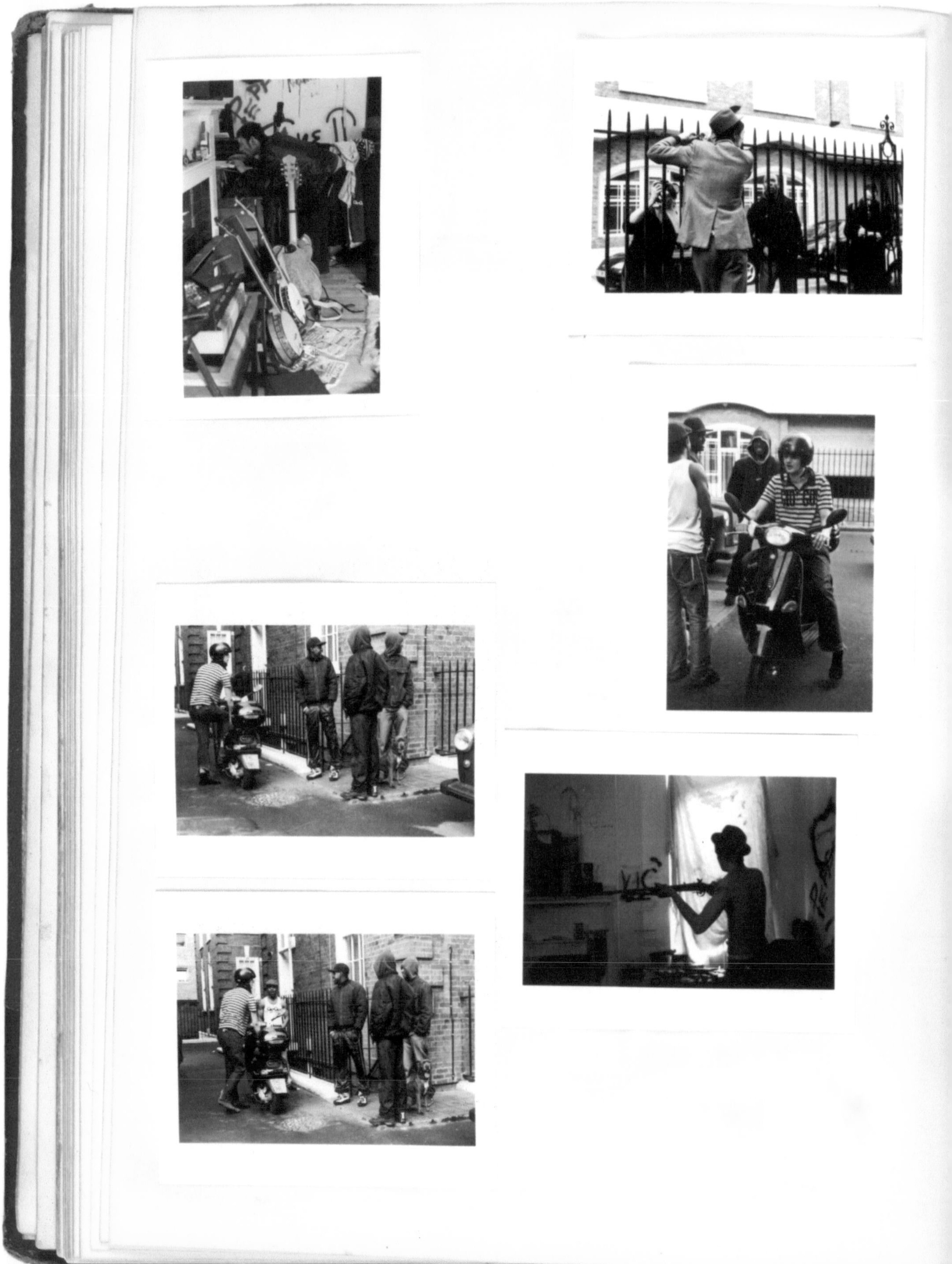

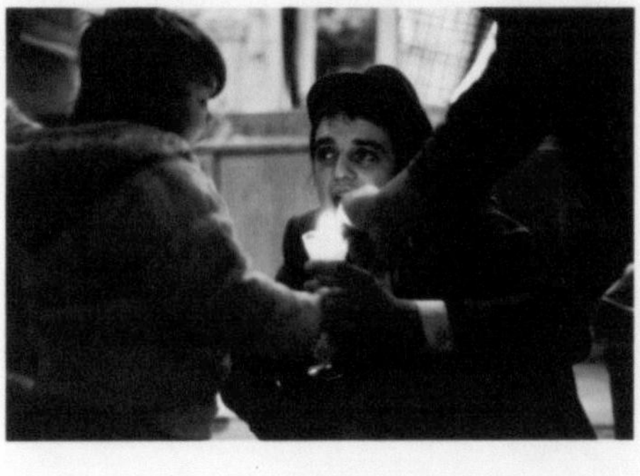

[redacted]

[redacted]te a line of poetry again.

To find contemporary resonances of Arthur Rimbaud we don't have to look very far. Pete Doherty's drug fuelled creativity is on the front of tabloids and celebrity magazines, in the culture sections of broadsheets and on television in everything from the national news to the late review. Doherty's honest acknowledgement of his drug use has opened out the debate on the subject, showing "drugs are for mugs" sloganeering to be a simplistic reaction to activity that is now epidemic throughout many different social groups in our society.

...uality of Doherty's music dependent

[redacted]Doherty's output as an artist is over shadowed by the overwhelming interest in his activity as a celebrity, and in this respect he differs greatly from his 19th century counterpart. Our perception of the work of a contemporary artist is so entwined with our perceptions of their public persona that it seems impossible to assess the work as separate from the celebrity. Modern artists are obliged to develop both aspects in parallel if they are to have any hope of recognition. Indeed some artists have acknowledged this development, and have shifted the focus of their practice entirely, and the celebrity in fact now becomes the artwork.

...baud had lit...

1 Saturday afternoon

One million at least many holes in the fire blanket cover the glushic and stare in and out of the cell window // Villein is still and static

Cold and 26

Did he somewhere along the way become more approachable – given the heavy horse's chaotic creation

it covers against regulations
3 times they came in the Yesterday

I'll lead you a merry dance
sick legal banter out on the vines where song like slang is slung like dead bed sheet snakes from cell to cell. 'E got a touch being H'd off'

For this is not old school parisian hell, but a slightly more sanitized one, and with a fresh lick of paint but they do that anyway.

I wasnt there for the reality
but christ knows you cant
whach the colours and shapes
of London in the 50's, buses
the cars and powerstations.
Villein had a tele in his cell
and sat sniffing on his bed
in his all-grey prison tracksuit
& thick socks as an old-time
Bobby blew the whistle on a
rogue in some anonymous flick
'Armed robbery in the Kings Cross area,
no trace of stolen property'
old films are like Nick really...
You see the same old faces with
a strange routine laced in nostalgia
What does Watney's brown ale taste
like – wondered Villein – and
how like the real read is the red
on the old reel that ~~we~~ we see the
buses move along in, and the
phone boxes sit still there in.
'The bogies'? Villein sniffed again
Metal cases full of money, that's
more the deal. Black white or skyblue
pink

2 Ladykiller

The lady was a girl was 23, french, a model – and – forgetting (impossible) being raped as a hostage in her own New York apartment some years before – a virgin.

In a Hackney flat some rugged blood sprayed lust took over the scene and she sucked Villein dry before letting him jack her up with smack & then – as he would rightfully have it – make love to her. Somehow they came together and the snowspeedballonsaneVillein thought of love for a while.

He sprayed a bloody heart on the white wall with the needle's backlog, just by where it said

'I ♥ D.V.D's' also in blood

She came back to London, having rejected him then, a year later and asked for a marriage.

The shadow of a long metal gate prolongs itself across the forecourt and across the yards of Morning. Villein mourns for the light and he's less contemplative and more ill than usual. Immune systems are all to cock and the fucking jangle of keys strangles my dreams.

'Coo-eee' came the voice of Methadone this morning, high pitched 'Young maaan!' like the little wobbly Enfield old ladies the nurse practised comic timing. The green juice works at the moment, enough Villein knew to get him naked save for socks to his flaps to reach the lime squid rectum

Simple things ~~occurred~~ to him: Where are my friends, my guitars, my family, my cars, my life'?

On the other side of the fences & gates and barbed shadows — Oh. Of course. Now this had been decided upon it was thought best to accumulate a list of definitive activities. What to do in this prison. Write? Why? And for who. All you need say is 'I'm in nick and its shite' Fuck the mystery, fuck the intrigue. cups of tea, Match of the day if your Peter* has a t.v, and smoke yourself to death.

3 Dress like Romans
act like Turks

So James is Hackney through 1 through 1 weirdly he's one of the few white fellas on the wing I'm now in. Turkish prevails. A few fellas Stoke Newington and Jimmy's end) of Hackney. He's here on a gun related matter. That was the one. At the flap — and his brother at the flap on the visit! haha villain listened

* cell

So really, Army paint tea,
and ethereal dreams about S. Andrews

3/4 The Scouser and the Turk

A non violent – save for the dramatic violence of raised voices – row rares up betwixt a Scouser and a Turkish prisoner. The turk's on a 15 year sentence for apparantly doing fuck all. The Scouser is reminding him what he did exactly. Headbutting. Villein goes to twinkle toes step away from the scene but the burly bald Turk appeals to him 'your name?'

'Villein'

'So... again...

I in Turkey and I paid to look for someone in London... Am I a murderer? Huh?' ~~'Huh'~~?'

Villein catches his grey blue eyes in a snapshot of prison oblivion. They smile together

'I should bleedin' well say not... ah lunch! ...'

The scouser's head turns to a deeply disturbing tray of 'jacket potatoes' ...

5 The Stroller

'I've strolled so many places in my mind' lazily blowing out smoke, slightly cherry flavoured out flakes the screwer give Villein ember or so. He was imagining walking up and down his cell but couldn't really see the point, exercise or not.

Villein yawned and flicked a pick of cotton off of his blanket that had been cropped from the inside of his tracksuit bottoms. Something was rearing up inside him now, as the Methadone script weakened and reality played its part in reality.

Strolling from the shower to his cell he'd had the nurse in fits when he was asked 'Cleaner now Villein?'

'Yeah i'm going the cinema in a few hours, i've got to look my best'

How ludicrous the idea must've seemed to Villein's nigga nurse to have him guffawing so. That the notion of being at liberty to go to the pictures should cause such hilarity is eery, alarming and sad. Oh lordy, see me through, I can't write about distant drills & fireblankets forever...

musikexpress
MIT CD Fiona Apple + The Fall + Calexico / Iron & Wine + Martha Wainwright + Broken Social Scene + Vashti Bunyan + Walking Concert + Reubens Accomplice + Jeffrey & Jack Lewis + Maritime
www.musikexpress.de
ATTAC!!! DIE 100 BESTEN POLITSONGS
The Darkness + Beastie Boys + Seeed + The Fall + Robbie Williams + Louis XIV +++
BABYSHAMBL
Pete Doherty und seine Band abseits der Skanda
Baggage
Reisegepäck
Checked Baggage
Austria
Checked

Sought in the blindness of
human comparison – the straight
playing goodhearted types who
wouldn't renege on their beliefs
for all the tea in town &
right up to the podium retouch
humanity. Lop their heads off
and they'd still mutter words
of love as their nerves wiggle the
tongue to still

Filthough
beautifully little
book of hearts will
your pages fall open
~~upon~~ ready (or as good as)
upon
sentiments rare & and
revealing the much clouded
blank pink page.

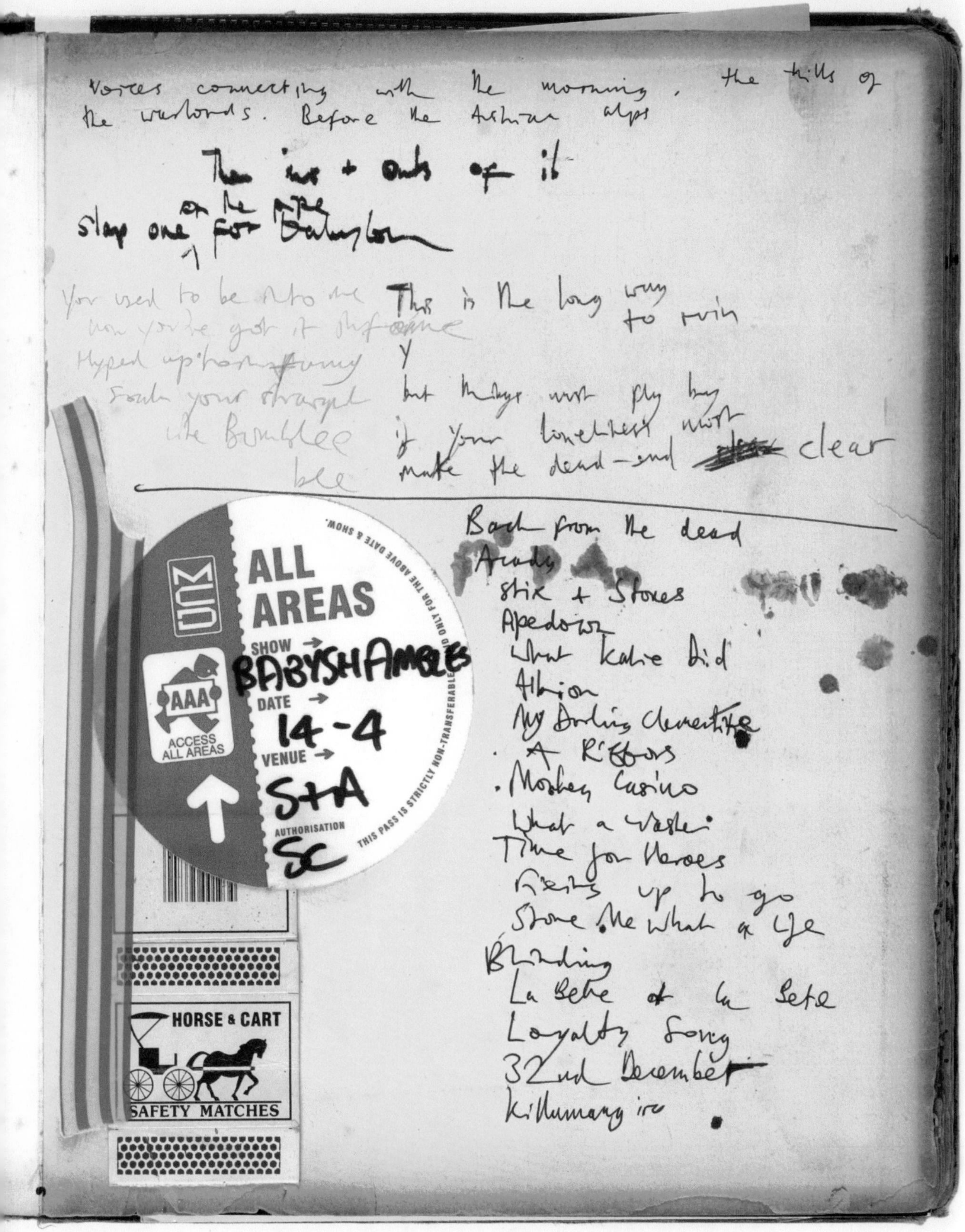
voices connecting with the morning, the hills of
the warlords. Before the Ashram alps
The ins + outs of it
Slap one for Babylon
on the pipe
You used to be into me
now you've got it
Hyped up
like Bumblee
bee
This is the long way
to ruin
but things won't fly by
if your loneliness won't
make the dead-end clear
Back from the dead
Arcady
Stix + Stones
Apedown
What Katie Did
Albion
My Darling Clementine
A Rebours
Monkey Casino
What a Waster
Time for Heroes
Fixing up to go
Stone Me What a Life
Blinding
La Belle et la Bête
Loyalty Song
32nd December
Killamangiro
ALL AREAS
SHOW →
BABYSHAMBLES
DATE →
14-4
VENUE →
S+A
AUTHORISATION
SC
AAA
ACCESS ALL AREAS
THIS PASS IS STRICTLY NON-TRANSFERABLE & VALID ONLY FOR THE ABOVE DATE & SHOW.
HORSE & CART
SAFETY MATCHES

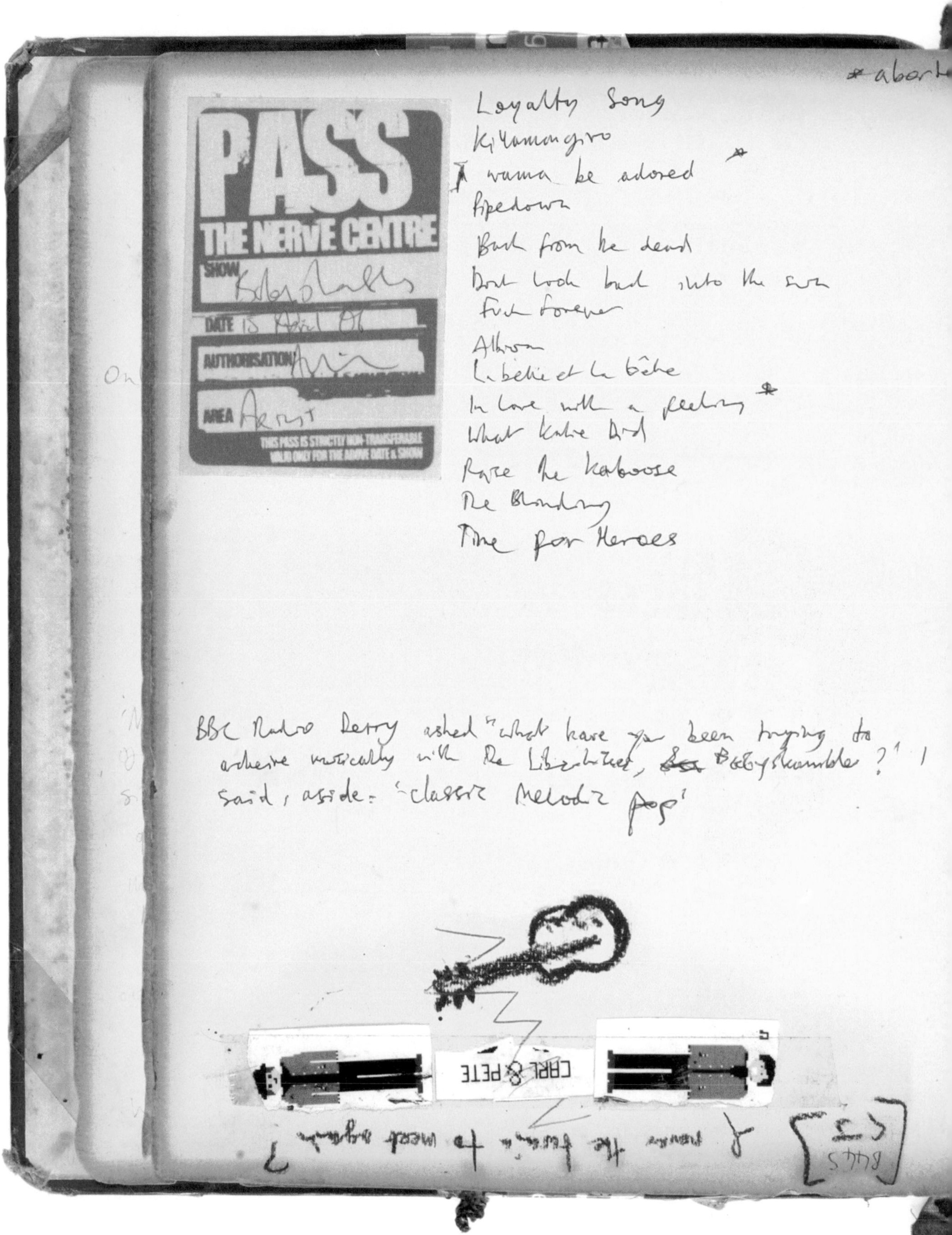
PASS
THE NERVE CENTRE
SHOW Babyshambles
DATE 15 April 06
AUTHORISATION
AREA Artist
THIS PASS IS STRICTLY NON-TRANSFERABLE
VALID ONLY FOR THE ABOVE DATE & SHOW
Loyalty Song
Kilamangiro
* wanna be adored *
Pipedown
Back from the dead
Don't look back into the sun
Fuck forever
Albion
La belle et la bête
In love with a feeling *
What Katie did
Raze the Kaboose
The Blinding
Time for Heroes
BBC Radio Derry asked "what have you been trying to achieve musically with the Libertines, ~~Bab~~ Babyshambles?" I said, aside: 'classic melodic pop'
CARL & PETE

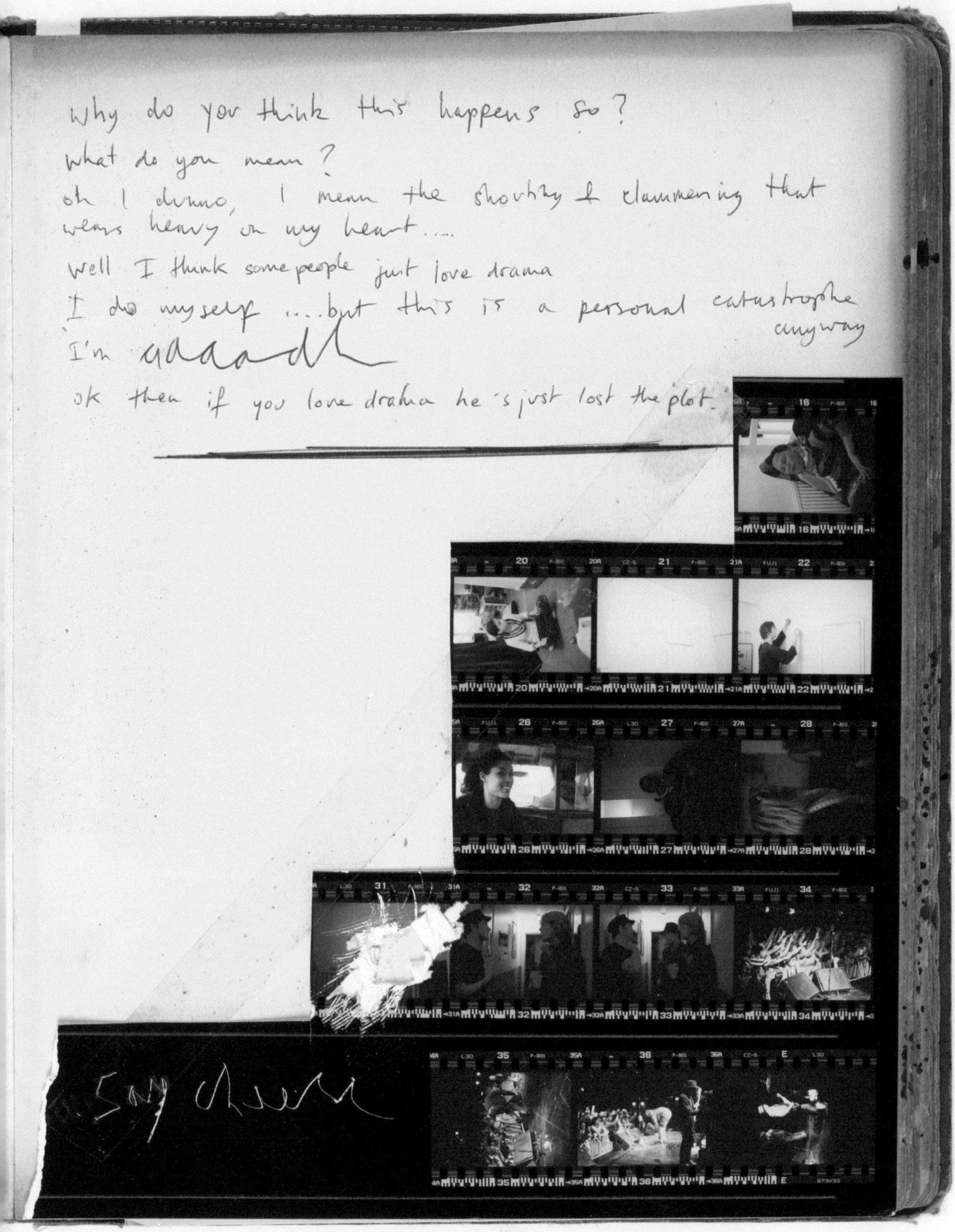
why do you think this happens so?
what do you mean?
oh I dunno, I mean the shouting & clammering that
wears heavy on my heart....
well I think some people just love drama
I do myself ....but this is a personal catastrophe
anyway
I'm aaaaah
ok then if you love drama he's just lost the plot.

Look into the eye of a half of a no-shower ... I'm a many of things: singer, dinger, minger, malingerer but I ain't a cab driver or a punctual tour manager type. So get me to the world on time or expect the worst. Dublin ... I'm sorrier than a pathetic excuse but for what besides meself? For letting anyone down down, mostly my band & the kids and then myself and my mothers nation, So forget me or go on, forgive me, forgive me. I need your best thoughts so much

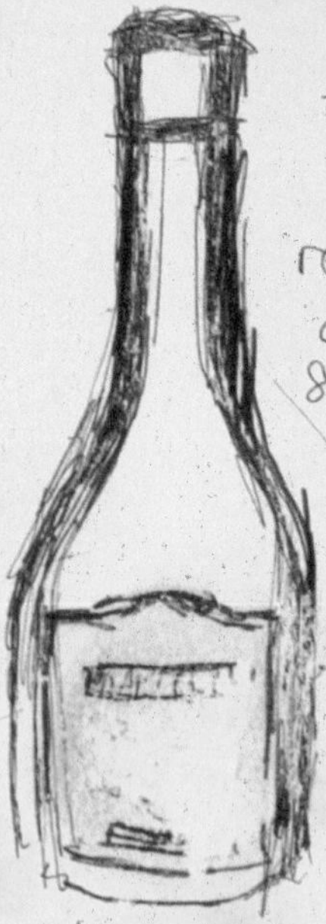

Opposite us
Eyeless A-list? wreckless
and for now (he lies a limb
reckless & (st)roll the dozen with
demi-monde which means less th
some sense fractious six kite &
a suburban green park. Restless
forgotten beneath reasons & deman
what is on offer is something
neither musical nor revolutionary.
Celebrate: pages & pages of
senders mostly & unfortunately
true to life. Written for its own
sake. clearly the written accompanies
to a wasteful existence. Magistrate:
"Mr Doherty, you have continued to live a
wilfully dissolute lifestyle" Implacable hatred
1/2 an hours hard labour
The boy couldn't possibly have looked
at Tommy anyway, sideways etc.
sullen spike haired hoodlums? Cheeky mop-haired
chaps
recrimination, booze & smack

Whistles shrieking up to the scarred arms blo
crashing out blood floods pale ripped masks
& no questions answered, let alone asked.
Putting paid to the pipe dreams of t.v
executives & their roll calls & snapping at
the early rising crew filming the filming film

Genial.

so Jen, am I a genius & you want both us?

Dingers forever

JJM 1
KODAK 400VC

On the way to Amsterdam, feeling
calm, together & fairly smart
at Heathrow. A nice, quiet day
relatively anyway. Sally sorted
out all the flights and I
am sat in the bar at Heathrow
A Gin & Tonic & cigarette
or two. Splendid. The only way
to travel... Outside the
bar & my head, the real world
carry's on in its carnage &
I oblivious to the current
furore concerning the alleged
'Administering a noxious substance'
photographs in the gutter press

Lennon by P. D

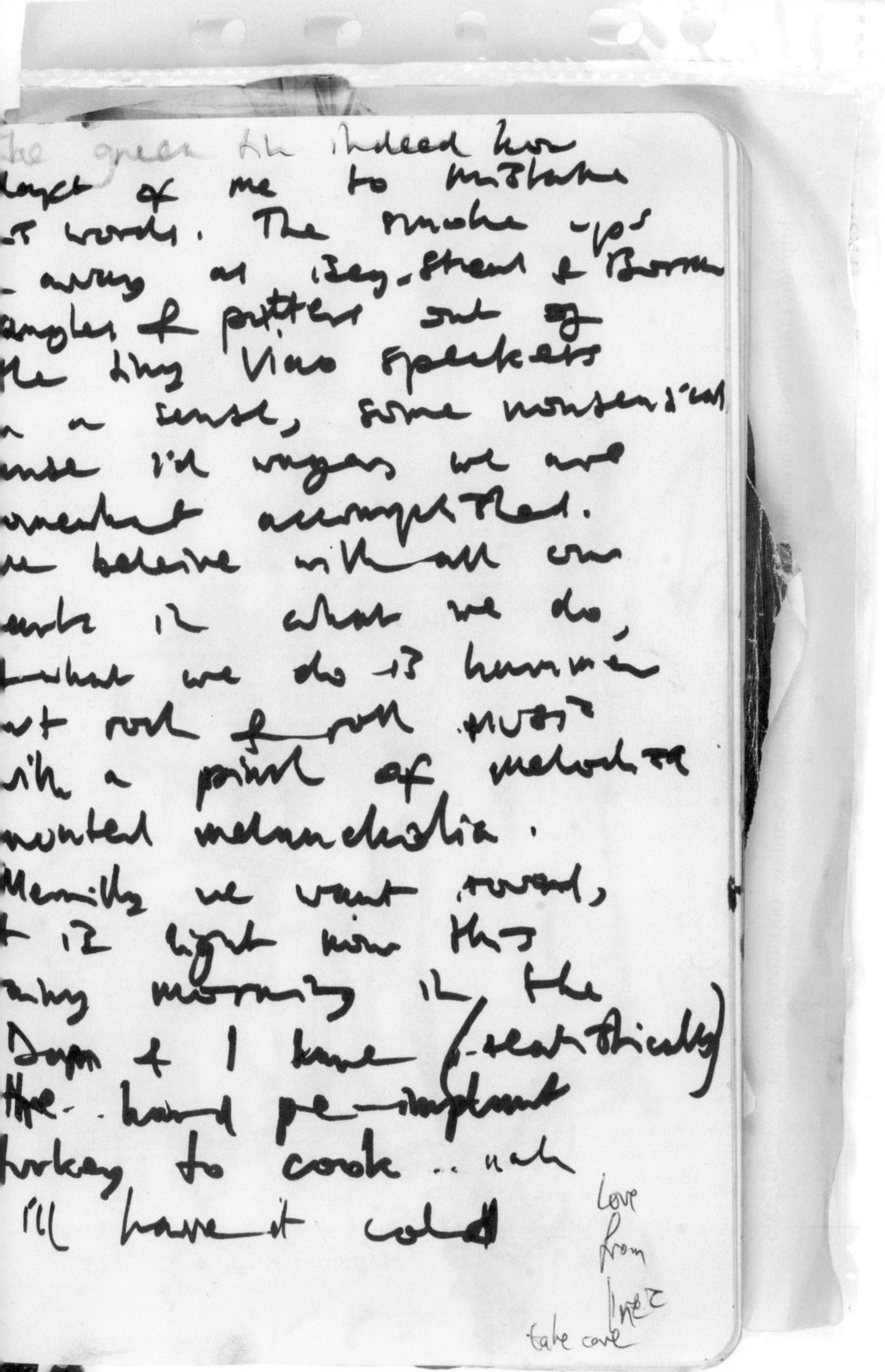
The green indeed how
of me to mistake
words. The smoke ups
away at Bay-Street & Bourn
angles & patters out of
the tiny Vias speakers
a sense, some nonsensical
I'd wager we are
somewhat accomplished.
believe with all our
hearts in what we do,
what we do is humane
rock & roll music
with a point of melodic
mounted melancholia.
Mentally we want reward,
it is light now this
morning is the
Day & I have (realistically)
the hard pre-implant
turkey to cook .. nah
I'll have it cold
Love
from
take care

lazy time it was for a panic station, all the shambles (post-put (?) blue-eyed era) plus one professor of smack & one darlin' of a 'form manager' in the shape of Sally Anchassi. Tommy Headlock is, needless to say, very much here and all ... indispensible if only for his amazing trick of continually turning up uninvited.
No smoke without a pipe & all o' that. God forgive me for even bringing up the allegations somewhat discarded now by time, not always so lazy, indeed the latest tabloid palaver has my very self same Bilo meself that I be am – has

me down as a wicked Svengali / Harold Shipman type character who 'administered noxious substances' into unconscious young ladies. 'These are serious allegations Mr Doherty' the officers from Scotland Yard's specialist crime unit did not fail to keep reminding me. Get this: Danny & Pearl received a visit from Scotland Yard – Pearl was asked if she recalled being 'fixed up with heroin' by Peter Doherty in nightclub toilets years ago . . . . oh dear, a little worrying –

not least because its not true but that is kind of irrelevant do you not agree?

V.A.T. No. 677 9797 38 Box Office Tel: 0870 112 1967

chapter one

Villein tramped up Englefield Rd, shirtless in light PPQ jeans and black converse. His lower arms skinny but chest bulging. He stepped into a bust up phone booth & had a sly pipe. He breathed deeply and ran his finger along broken glass. The sun warmed his upper body & a bead of sweat ran down the groove of a scar and popped

itself on a plastic spike
that stalagtited off his
prison Rosary. He was
on his way to probation,
with a rendezvous to
keep along the way.
He passed through Greys Mount
flats and saw Salt, a
black youth on a bike
speeding past. 'Villein'
came the salute
'Rude boy' replied polite
Villein and waved. Salt
spun around and they
touched. Villein squinted
in the sun.
'Aint live, Villein' said Salt.
'Aint been busy boy, I'm
with' it down mate, yeah
boy'

In a small room inside Villein
sat still like a mannequin with
a plastic swab sticking
out of his mouth, he
pulled it out eventually and
popped it into the test tube
Julie held out. She sighed.
'You look awful' she said
'Thankyou Julie' He replied
'There's nothing I can say is
there?' you won't be told.
You know, working in Hackney
I deal with real people with
real problems. People from
real disadvantaged backgrounds.
Villein frowned and spat back
'oh yeah? I imagine you do,
What do you want me to say
to that. You want my help?"

Villem smiled and they chatted awhile. Blues caught up with them in a blacked out Fiat. Villem jumped in and scored a fistful, a trouserful of Rocks & B. He jumped out outside the National Probation Service office. Julie Gibson was at the door, scowling at the Fiat as it pulled off
'On time for a change Villem'...
Villem feigned indignation and kissed the lady inappropriately on the cheek
'Hello Julie' he said

He left the NPS office
with a sour taste in his
mouth and stopped a
passing taxi. He piped
up in the back, and
sank into his seat.
3 minutes later the car
pulled up outside Laburnum St
(the west end of). He
scaled the railings & skipped
around to his flat.
The door was unlocked
and he crashed through
it. He wasted no time.
He reached into his
kecks and pulled out
a plastic bag full of
balls. He passed the
bathroom and smiled at
the cat having a shit.

'Gangsta!' said Jonny Headlock, looking up from the laptop. He was downloading stuff onto Limewire. 'Immortal Technique & Kalashnikov.

Villem stepped over a skinny girl panting as she lay on the floor. 'Bonjour' they said to each other.

Straight onto the fav white leather sofa . . . his favourite long-stemmed spoon was already caked in damp filters. He emptied a bag of brown & 1/3 of a bag of white into it and squirted some water to top it up. He sprinkled some vitamin C

powder into the silver
trinket and crushed
it altogether with the
arse end of clean
dinger (needle).
He heated up proceedings
with a cheap green
lighter. An aroma of
exquisite recall breezed
into his face and
senses. He set the
trinket a'balance and
looked at his arm.
He flinched, took a
leather belt from the
floor and then filled
the dinger in spurts
from the spoon.

Chapter TWO

Villiers sat shirtless & shoeless in his little room at the priory. He was in 2 minds whether or not to lay upon his bed or wander on downstairs for a fag & a crisp sandwich -

He was showered & bathed & finally smelling sweet rather than clammy & sweat'd as of before, from seemingly endless groups & a supervised walk round the lake.

It stings when I sing,
and its not stings like
just to rush f fuck
knock out the clock

my days are spent
swerving prongs
like old bill in a jag
but reality keeps on like a nag
"stop it stop it stop it" before
you cop it"
cop it being worse things than
a sting... cop it being
worse than verses that
appear in the morning too unforgiving
to sing, and there's not much
worse than that thing except
perhaps death! cop it is death,
a blood red card from God if
he were a ref

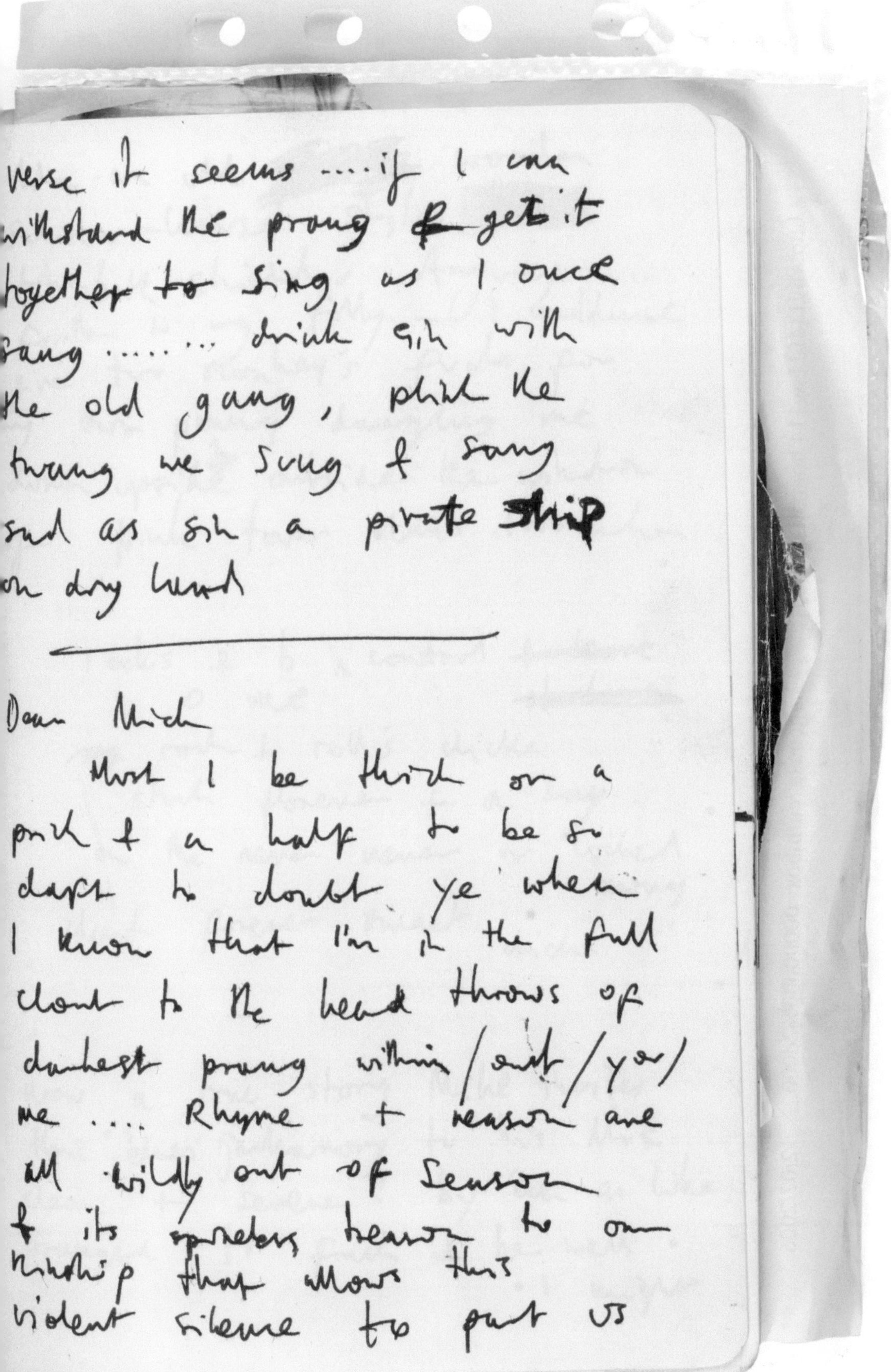
verse it seems ....if I can
withstand the prong get it
together to sing as I once
sang .... drink gin with
the old gang, pluck the
twang we sung & sang
sad as sin a pirate ship
on dry land

Dear Mick
Must I be thick or a
prick & a half to be so
daft to doubt ye when
I know that I'm in the full
clout to the head throws of
darkest prang within/out/you/
me .... Rhyme + reason are
all wildly out of season
& its spineless treason to our
mateship that allows this
violent silence to part us

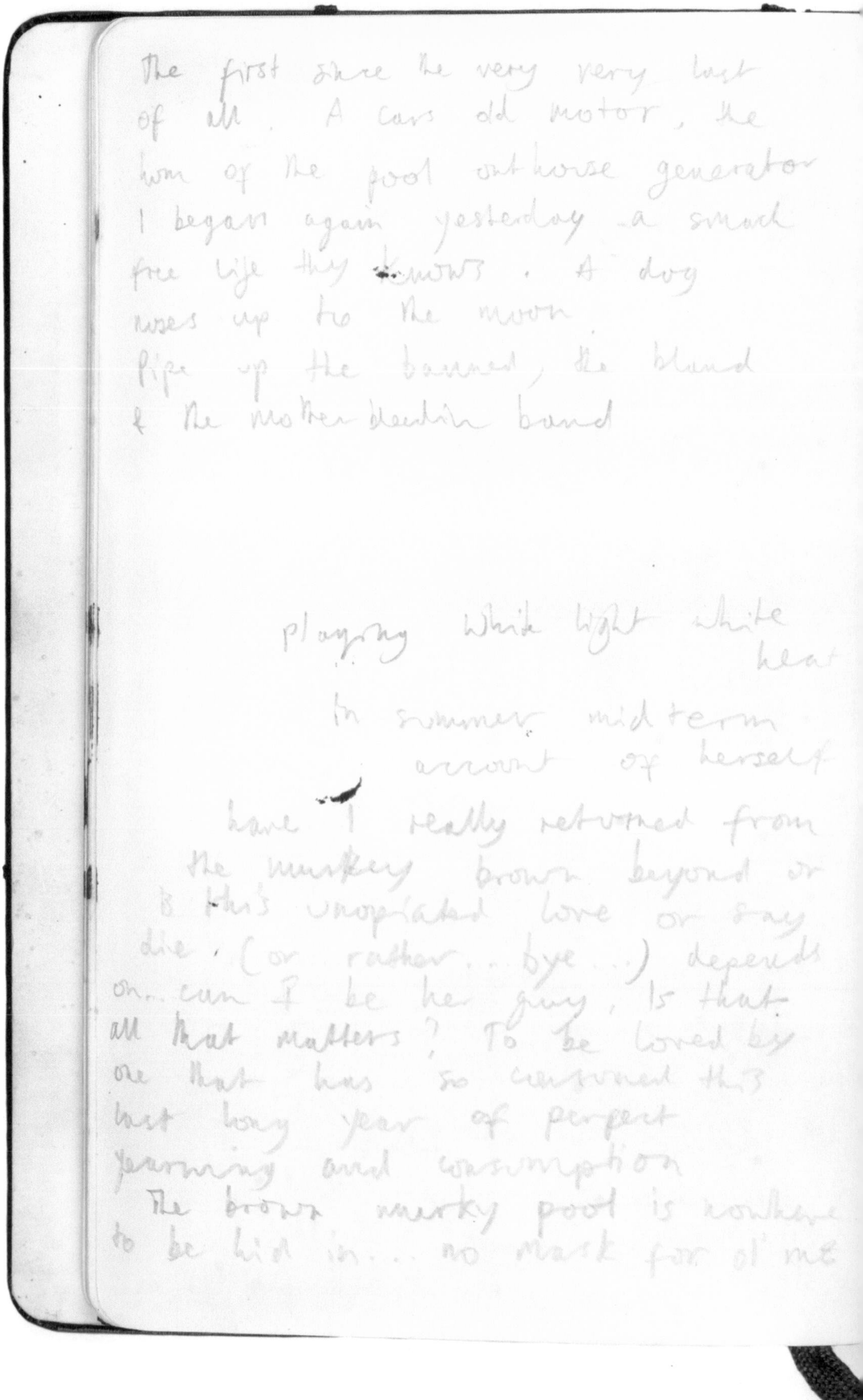

The first since the very very last
of all. A cars old motor, the
hum of the pool outhouse generator
I began again yesterday a small
free life they knows. A dog
rises up to the moon
Pipe up the banned, the bland
& the mother-bleedin band

playing White light white
heat

In summer midterm
account of herself

have I really returned from
the murkey brown beyond or
is this unrequited love or say
die, (or rather... bye...) depends
on... can I be her guy, Is that
all that matters? To be loved by
one that has so consumed this
last long year of perfect
yearning and consumption
The brown murky pool is nowhere
to be hid in... no mask for ol' me

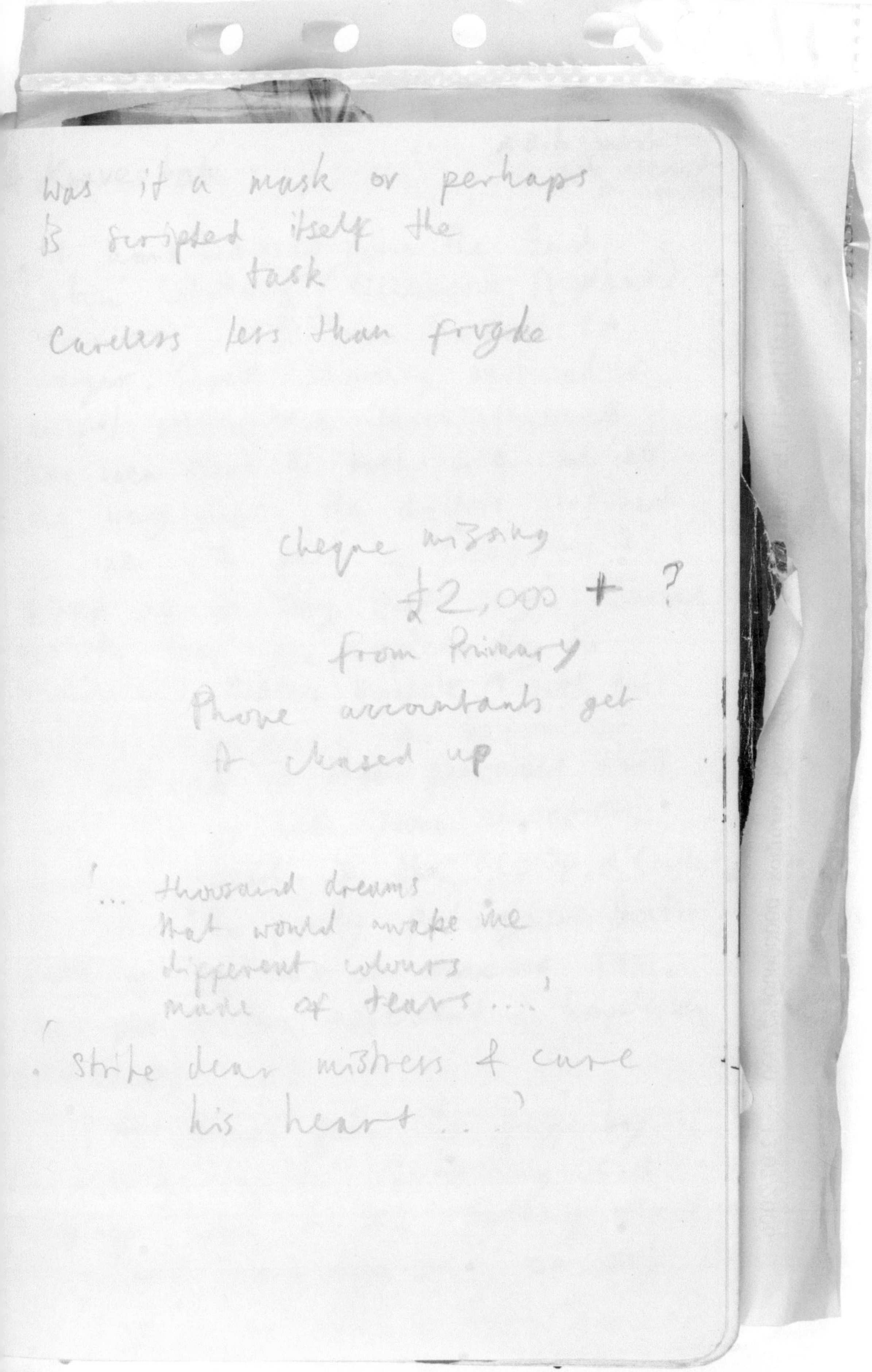

Was it a mask or perhaps
Is scripted itself the
task

Careless less than fragile

cheque missing
£2,000 + ?
from Primary
Phone accountants get
it chased up

'... thousand dreams
that would awake me
different colours
made of tears ....'

'Strike dear mistress & cure
his heart ...'

A Knave's tale

*n.b must get internet in country

I have returned from the 2nd Lisbon Lobotomy (Naltrexone Implant) mission ... with some success I'd wager. Stout, stunning musical & misfit accomplice Mick Whitnall has been there & back with me all the way down the doctor's stitched up line. The pair of skagfree & fixed up to stay that way. I hope not to bore you sufficiently to down the Albion bookle * with this nagging dependence on heroin or life without it that pervades this tome. It is with some elevation that I remark on the 'Coup d'Carlos' (he being the portly portuguese Doctor full of wisdoms & maxims for the use of the afflicted & hopelessly addicted)

I am drawn from the page by the heavily rapid stuttering c.d playing here in the potting shed its going 'nag nag nag' or 'say say say' or something from some

version of bootlegged Sister Ray
truly back in the day
'sucking on my ding dong'

There was one huge fucker of a nurse I recall in the midsts of sedated withdrawals tying me up to the bed again & all that nonsense. Mick went right through it and out the other side .... huge grazes on his arms from struggling with the cotton plastic strips they force you down with .. found at times in the wardrobe searching for some lost piece of crack.

After shuddering through hell an' all we got the implants banged in and stumbled away from the 'hospital' place with its peacocks and birds in plume and long line of senile residents. Days in window shut out sunny rooms fighting for dear life. We made it to a hotel (finally – really, these eventide currency quibbles) & after a night of existential desperation & eventually climbing into the bed of Sir Whitnall and

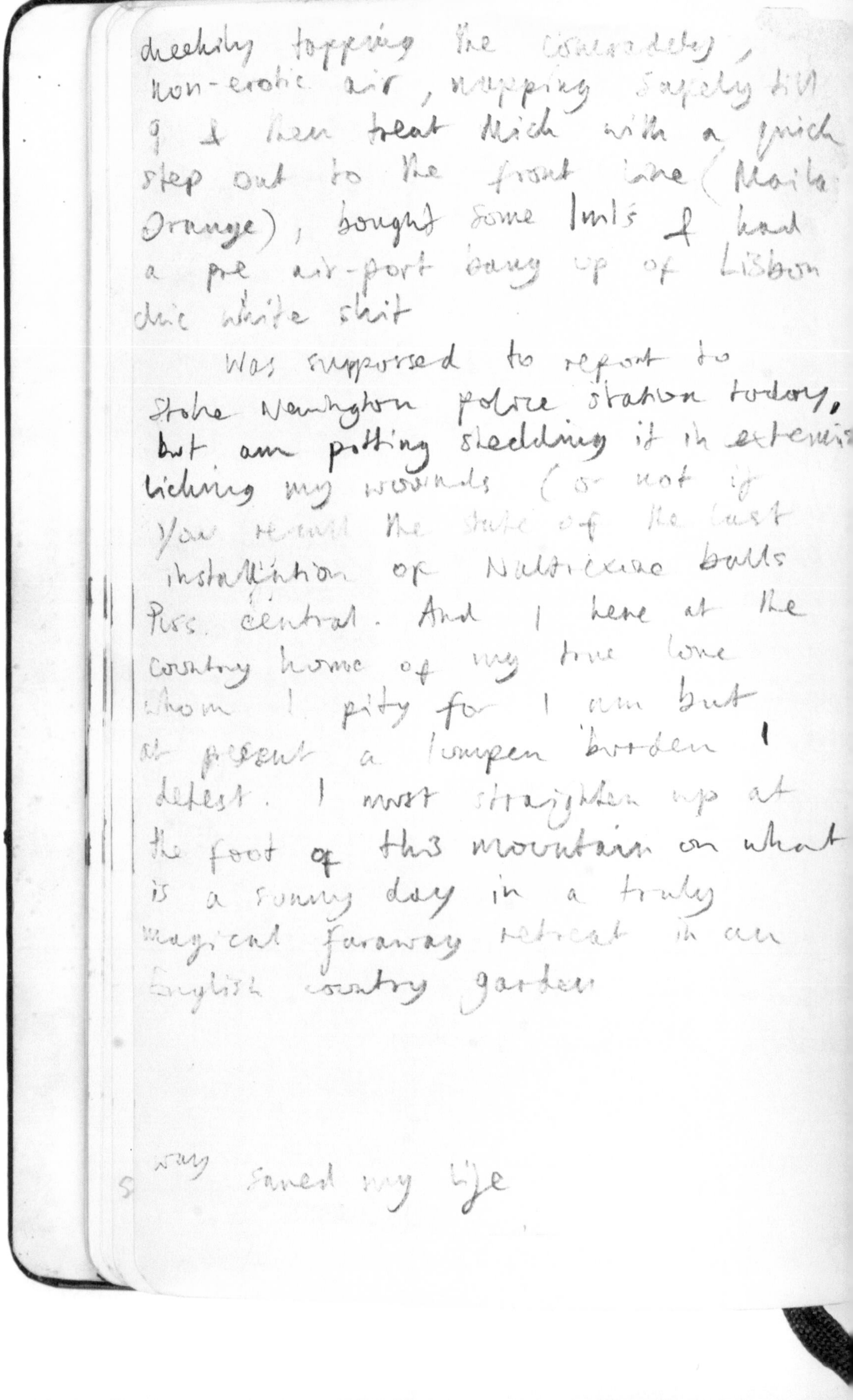
cheekily topping the comradeley,
non-erotic air, napping safely till
9 & then treat Mich with a quick
step out to the front line (Maida
Orange), bought some limes & had
a pre air-port bang up of Lisbon
chic white shit
Was supposed to report to
Stoke Newington police station today,
but am putting shedding it in extemis
licking my wounds (or not if
you recall the state of the last
installation of Nublicure balls
Pass central. And I here at the
country home of my true love
whom I pity for I am but
at present a lumpen burden I
detest. I must straighten up at
the foot of this mountain on what
is a sunny day in a truly
magical faraway retreat in an
English country garden

way saved my life

PRIORY
Visitor

Me, Wolfie
+ General

I'm thinking 'c'mon dont fuck about'
I'm so ungrateful. Biding my
insane time to count down & lift
off and what not and whenever it
works. Doubt not my integrity but
the course of my actions leaves
authorities livid & distrustful, then
again they could have me if they
so desired. Bang up. Still, the law
is the law and cant be denied though
still I try so & the strike me down
each stand I take, still pushing my
hand ... they can take me & make me
but til' they really break me or the
turn, as the wheel yearns to cycle

Years ago I'd have said the
very same, 'at any cost' 'I'll sit it
out' etc etc but only back then it was
all about the brown

Wide-eyed boy in freefall, through
the clouds and oh god I'm impatient
Sort us out, missus, eh? eh?
She makes a racket, that's how it's
her you know its so ... perlease?
C'mon C'mon
You know we got a good thing going on
C'mon c'mon we really got a good thing
going on

The disarray around me belies (else I lie) a fairly sound & tidy state of mind. My dear sweet love would appear to be in somewhat of a rage perhaps due to my being decamped to the potting shed this cold rainy night and her having a pop thusly: (I having claimed to be 'working on songs') 'You're sat here in your hovel in your own shit, wallowing in self indulgence.' The Lord ~~has~~ knows it's a ~~continued cruelly faulted dialogue~~ consistent response that occurs to her to air. Any time I might stop, write, strum & 'indulge' a creative urge I am naught but a vainglorious swine & a cunt of the highest order. Oh what nonsense I nervously scrawl in the dark dark country night. The air clean & sweet & sharp to the taste. My mind has always made mountains out of molehills and tonight the very silence itself conjures up

a foreboding, and a tense chill
about my body. The boiler room is
my close/noisy neighbour & the
the wind (my other neighbour) she
thunders up at the contoral wall
every now ~~&~~ then with dreadful
interruptions. The wind is not so
cocky tonight, having had a hard few
~~time lately~~ weeks of it he is
musing & punny ... Deliberating ... and
perhaps deciding ...... so free is he.
At ease with the infinite seas & skies,
or whipping up frenzy itself into
mental weather.
Such A storm ~~is~~ has the Albion (that
sturdy ghost ship) sailed through
I'd say recent-lay. Not often gently
has the good night concluded its
business with me. Mostly my own
worst enemy is to be blamed for
all the palavas, but I ~~can~~
think of a few other contenders.

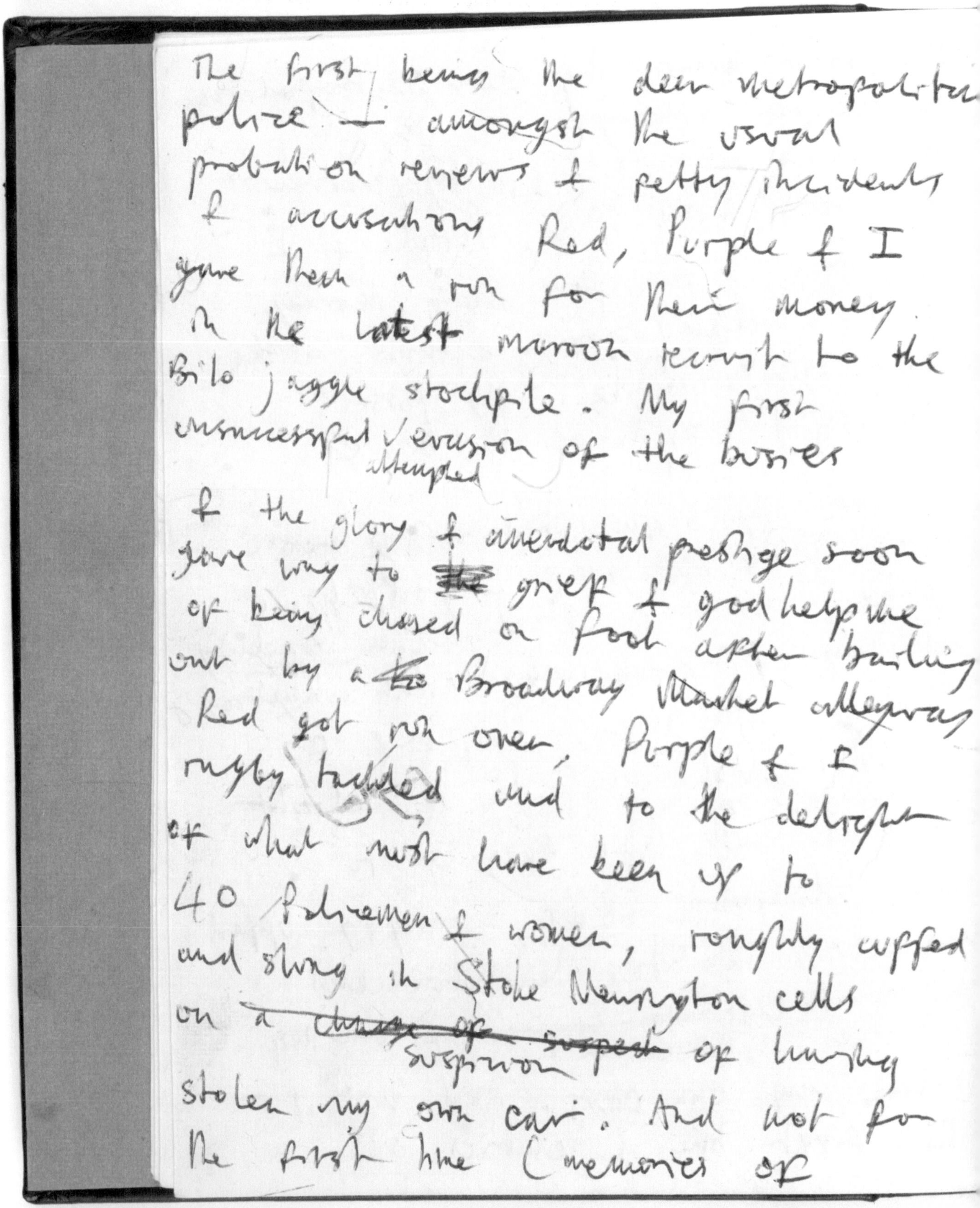

The first being the dear Metropolitan
police — amongst the usual
probation reviews & petty incidents
& accusations Red, Purple & I
gave them a run for their money
in the latest maroon recruit to the
Bilo jaggle stockpile. My first
unsuccessful attempted evasion of the busies

& the glory & anecdotal prestige soon
gave way to ~~the~~ grief & god help me
of being chased on foot after bailing
out by a ~~the~~ Broadway Market alleyway
Red got run over, Purple & I
rugby tackled and to the delight
of what must have been up to
40 policemen & women, roughly cuffed
and slung in Stoke Newington cells
on a ~~charge of~~ ~~suspect~~ suspicion of having
stolen my own car. And not for
the first time (memories of

bombing it to Birmingham in
a beautiful old grey thing with
2 boys from the crew .. plans to
see my first Pretty Pretty Things
gig scuppered by West Midlands
police insistence that I'd nicked
me own car. The cheek!)
Anyway, they may throw the book
at Red who has 99 previous convictions
many involving mechanically propelled
vehicles and specifically evading
arrest. Something of a ~~speciality~~
speciality I can reliably inform you,
having sat gawping many a time
as Redovan ~~& I~~ rolls out ~~countless~~
tales from his eventful ~~[illegible]~~ past!) A
love affair with reckless adventure, as
she sometimes calls herself. Trouble or
so. Anyway, I meant to explain
how such carnage is not actually
my desire, nor the filth &
empty wandering that makes up most

of my life. For now I am not directly under seige or at someones proffessional disposal. I mean to say it is the end of a certain era. I can sense its almost ceremonial conclusion... in the recent signing of a record contract as Babyshambles for EMI. Also, I have been informed that my behaviour reached an all time low during the recent visit to Thailand with booze, downers & dingers fuelling a no-nonsense nonsensical declaration of war upon my most respected values such as dignity, refinement and subtelty (subtleness)? — and composure in the face of confrontation, & confusion ..... after deportation I was thinking along the lines of being single. Folly such a thought, my heart aching & swimming & I dearly missing Kate despite being convinced that the relationship was an unbearable & intolerable disaster. However impractical my ~~at~~ raging drug addiction upon matters is not really up for debate but still I found myself incapable of justifying all the pain & general dysfunction of much of the affair.

And so, I flee / am booted out ... and this time I'm conscious of something or some<u>one</u> in myself having gone away: To sustain any standard or living or a hope for the morrow I must be done with certain behaviours, I write this expecting to hear a sneering response such is my confidence in this area — and yet part of me retains a contradictory belief that I can learn from the shame & strain of my awfulness & become a better man by default. There's hope for us all, right? Why not.

And so I remain in the freezing climes of church farms potting shed scribbling away and attempting to tidy up amidst a wee tiff with

the birthday girl. I have been banging
up I confess, and yet my use is
extremely moderate ~~&~~ and controlled
~~?~~ What am I saying? Kate will not
tolerate this shite I wouldn't blame
her, and alongside the fixing neither
of us seem to completely trust each
other although I love her and no
other and the tiffs & tumults
come ~~[illegible]~~ between magical
times. The most cherished & happy
those spent in her arms hours are
this suspended fued? ... So why
she certainly knows how to oh I dunno,
out of me. Or tears. get a rise
guitars. Or low-flying
Is it me trying to avoid
the reality of my most antisocial
habits, or is there any defence in
these debates that I am confidently
use. Perhaps not ... and so a sorry,
selfish cunt I might well be. I only
wish that this selfishness would properly
kick in and end all the confusion – as

mostly I am not digging spikes into myself but am a rejuvenated spirit and seeing the world and my love with wider, keener eyes. Such is the lay of the land. I have plans ... and yet ~~when~~ challenged I cling to half baked ideas about the situation. Writing this down is calming for me, in the misery of exile, Paradise Lost, doghorse etc. Sometimes it becomes impossible to conceive of even the most common-place of actions (such as standing up and going inside to warmth and a drink with a splendid array of characters)

It is divinity itself, true love, and hell is the ~~[illegible]~~ hearts terrible palpitations as a 'turning'. is in the offing. All I wish is for her to come and lead me back out of the dark. Hmm. I seem stuck on this matter — and still I mean

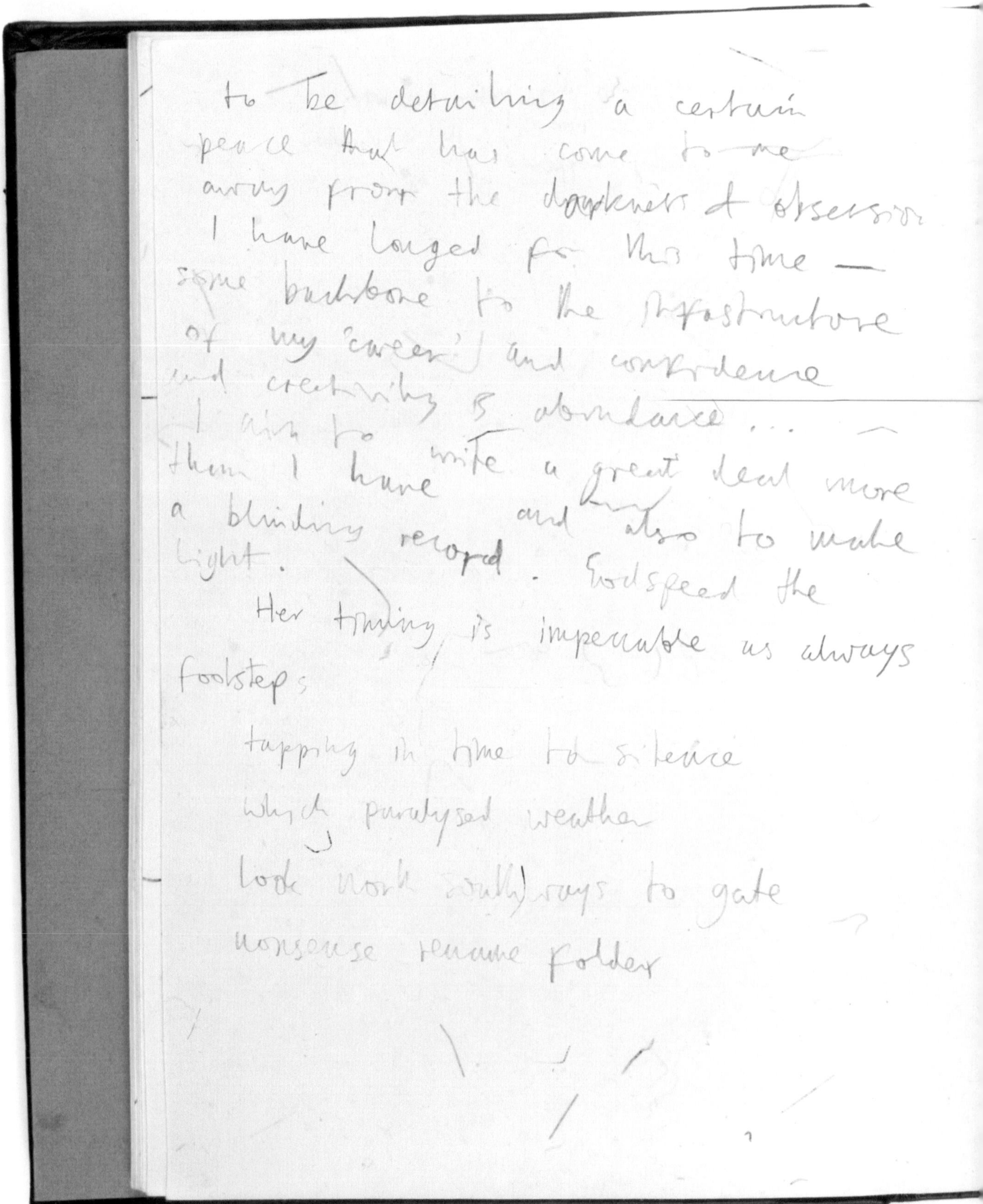

to be detailing a certain
peace that has come to me
away from the darkness & obsession
I have longed for this time —
some backbone to the infrastructure
of my 'career' and confidence
and creativity is abundance ...
I aim to write a great deal more
than I have and also to make
a blinding record. Godspeed the
light.

Her timing is impeccable as always
footsteps

tapping in time to silence
which paralysed weather
look north south ways to gate
nonsense rename folder

sleeping in the great river, the fan whirrs
all night & I'm not as uneasy as ever I
was the four blended colour frames come in and
out at me as does the jacket like laughter
from the smokers room. Mercy & denial ...
insane. Further tabloid infamy yesterday just
when I thought everything was too good to
be true. Some Australian arseholes have me on
camera phone banging up and apparently slagging
Kate off. Bang to rights I suppose although
to be fair I was in a hell of a state at
the time and we had fallen out.
Fuck it. The last few weeks together have
been so loving and so much positive looking
to the future & it makes me sick to my
heart but I must face it. I love the
girl so dearly and that's why I'm in this
fucking clinic isn't it? Another 36 hours clean
now and sticking to it this time I fancy.
Aboard the wagon balloon .....

3.00pm 29th Jan 2007

So there's a silent pop as I push the vein & launch a great shift into my system. Eye-closing, jaw tightening speedballing through the opening hours of my detox at the Nightingale Hospital, Lisson Grove.

It begins now, does the rest of my life

3.00 am 31st Jan 2007

and onwards, through time & these sterile corridors of the clinic you follow me. 36 hours in and not much to show in the way of withdrawals (only vomiting though that may have been the final line of shitty sparkling gak that I had concealed in my pillow) foolishly, before the very dawn

I medicate myself further and prolong the detox. Shall we say 7.00 am is the (first) of the brown stream, and a fuckin hootenanny it was indeed no mistake.
I have slept a great deal these few days and now vow to check out Friday (?) or 12 hours after my first clean opiate test... whichever comes sooner.
My eyes are apt to gander now, and another marathon dream stint is on the cards/. Being New York including one that has just this night passed ~~[illegible]~~ reoccurred — involving a picturesque French village and some manner of cultural exchange, in person & via cyberspace
It is hard to ~~[illegible]~~ write anything down when one is seeing double in this heavy lidded whir.

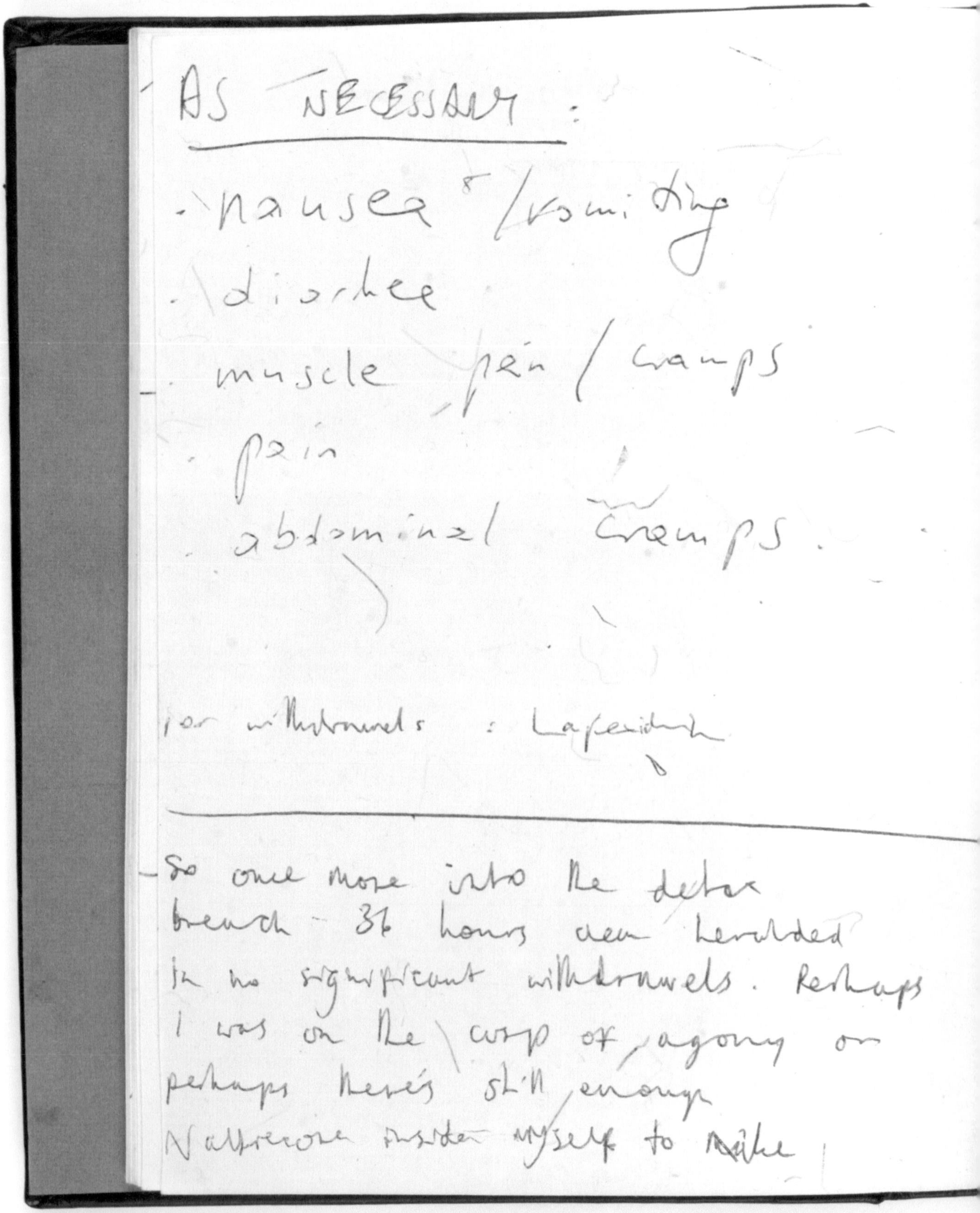

AS NECESSARY:

- nausea & / vomiting
- diarhee
- muscle pain / cramps
- pain
- abdominal cramps.

for withdrawels : Lapexidium

So once more into the detox breach – 36 hours clean heralded in no significant withdrawels. Perhaps I was on the cusp of agony or perhaps there's still enough Naltrexone inside myself to make

the dreaded turkey like warm rather
than cold as I have always
known it to be, For cold hard
agonies, torments & general ~~intense~~ intolerable
abominations upon my body and
mind. 'Waiting for the heartaches to
come' am I ~~?~~ now. For the time
being & in the meantime I sit
stupefied having made short work
of my final stashettes.
I now surrender to the science of
detoxification and pray that god
speeds the worst of it and
saturday morning at the latest
will see me once more in
my Love's loving arms. We have been
close this time passed and with
me smack & needle free we shall
marry in the summer and I
become ten times happier than any
given smackhead. Huzzah!

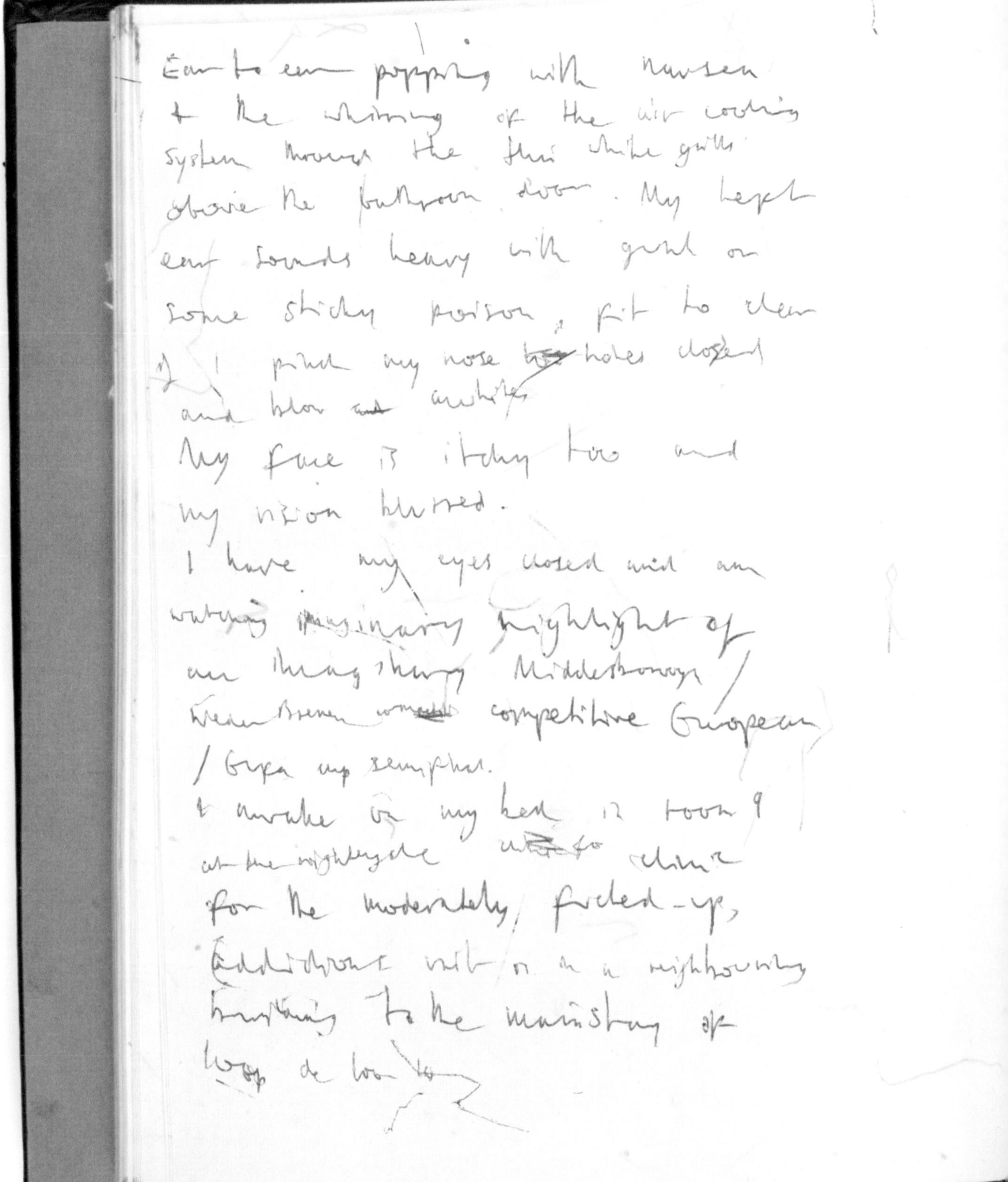

Ear to ear popping with nausea
& the whirring of the air cooling
system through the thin white grills
above the bathroom door. My left
ear sounds heavy with gunk or
some sticky poison, fit to clear
if I pinch my nose holes closed
and blow outwards
My face is itchy too and
my vision blurred.
I have my eyes closed and am
watching imaginary highlights of
our thingy Middlesbrough /
Steaua Bucuresti competitive European
/ Uefa cup semifinal.
I awake on my bed in room 9
at the Nightingale to clamour
for the moderately fucked-up,
Addictions unit on a neighbouring
building to the mainstay of
loop de loo

some ennui hustles its way into the small angular room, the pen is lead heavy and doubts and depressing notions guide my hand across the page like the credits in bold white that fall down the screen, a black & white picture of a chewed on wedding cake.

• A couple of hours of old comedy on D.VD for your detox pleasure. A flea bitten old cockney totter rows with his son, an embittered but hearty heir to the horse and cart.

Flat caps, crombies, old suits, neckerchiefs, trilbies, pork pies, rags - bones, old plugs and damn it all ... trinket mania.

coarse tongues, curious plots & cobblers.

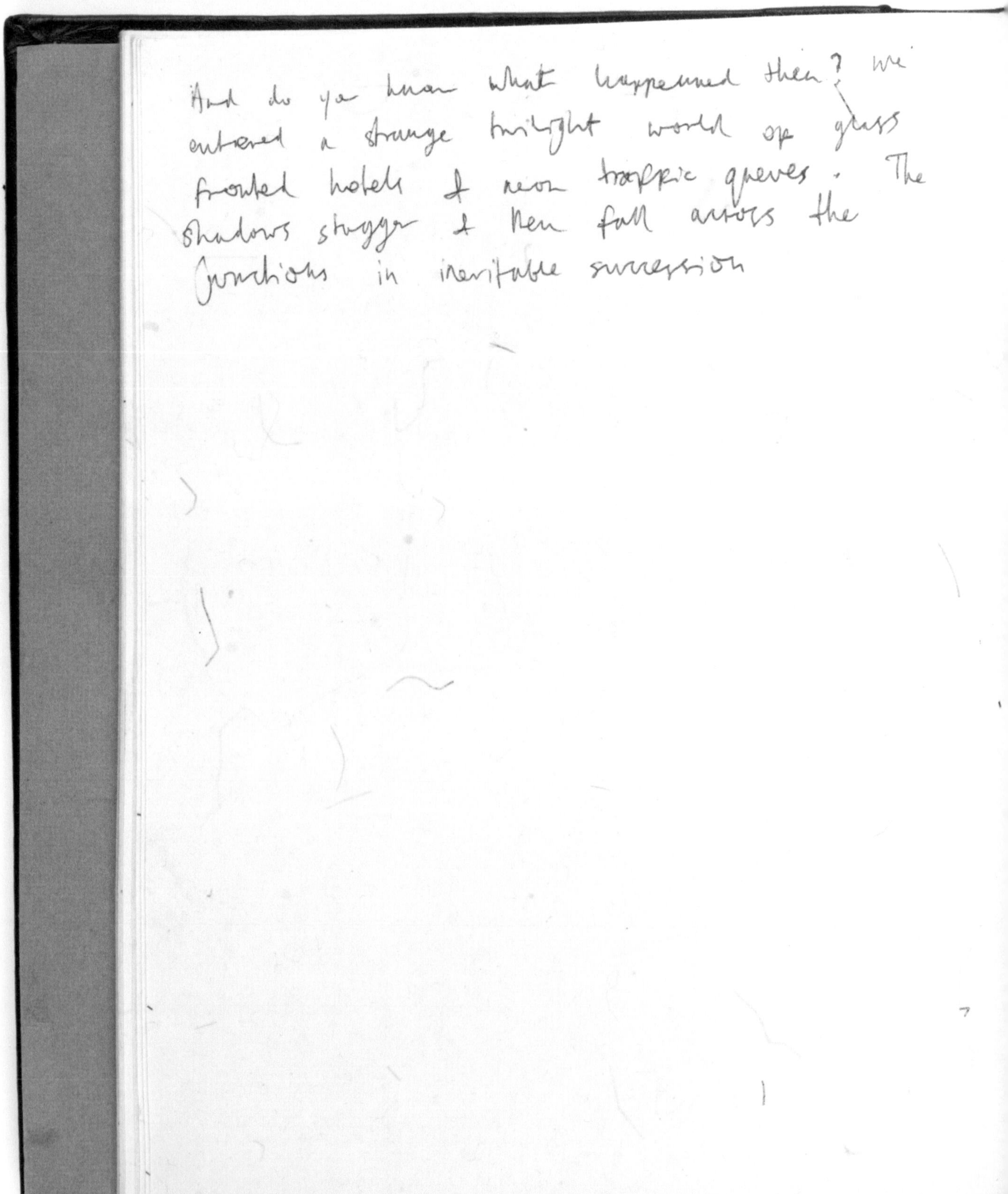

And do you know what happened then? We entered a strange twilight world of glass fronted hotels & neon traffic queues. The shadows stagger & then fall across the junctions in inevitable succession

EDITOR'S NOTES

Every effort has been made to fulfil requirements with regard to reproducing copyright material. The author and publisher will be glad to rectify any omissions at the earliest opportunity.

Note. Peter will often refer to himself as *bilo*, a childhood nickname given to him by his father.

Page 9 (upside down)
Lyrics to 'The Good Old Days'. Words and music by Peter Doherty and Carl Barât © 2002. Reproduced by permission of EMI Music Publishing Ltd/Rough Trade Music Ltd, London WC2H 0QY.

Pages 16 – 17
Detailing events of an argument in a pub between Peter's friends, Johnny of Britpop band Menswear and other individuals, over the owing of an amount of money.

Page 21
Lyrics to 'Music When the Lights Go Out'. Words and music by Peter Doherty and Carl Barât © 2004. Reproduced by permission of EMI Music Publishing Ltd/Rough Trade Music Ltd, London WC2H 0QY.

Pages 24 – 26
Memories of childhood, and the many locations Peter grew up in.

Page 57
Excerpt from 'A Diamond Guitar' by Truman Capote, reproduced by kind permission of the Penguin Group (UK), from *Breakfast at Tiffany's*, Hamish Hamilton, 1958. Copyright © Truman Capote, 1958.

The original text reads:
Except that they did not combine their bodies or think to do so, though such things were not unknown at the farm, they were as lovers. Of the seasons, spring is the most shattering: stalks thrusting through the earth's winter-stiffened crust, young leaves cracking out on old left-to-die branches, the falling-asleep wind cruising through all the newborn green. And with Mr. Schaeffer it was the same, a breaking up, a flexing of muscles that had hardened.

It was late January. The friends were sitting on the steps of the sleep house, each with a cigarette in his hand. A moon thin and yellow as a piece of lemon rind curved above them, and under its light, threads of ground frost glistened like silver snail trails. For many days Tico Feo had been drawn into himself – silent as a robber waiting in the shadows.

Page 59
Referring to Sasha, a schizophrenic prostitute who was living with Peter and Carl at the time. She later tried to kill Peter by stabbing him with a pair of scissors at the Prince Charles Cinema, Leicester Square, London.

Page 60
D. H. Lawrence 'The State of Funk', excerpt from *Phoenix II* (1968), reproduced by kind permission of Pollinger Limited and the Estate of Frieda Lawrence Ravagli.

Page 67
A jump to early 2002.

Page 70
After signing to Rough Trade, on the way to Nomis recording studio, to record some demos that will form the basis of the Libertines debut album.

Page 72
Lyrics to 'Up the Bracket'. Words and music by Peter Doherty and Carl Barât © 2002. Reproduced by permission of EMI Music Publishing Ltd/Rough Trade Music Ltd, London WC2H 0QY.

Pages 74 – 75
First British tour, and first feelings of pressure of being on the music industry conveyor belt.

Pages 94 – 95
Christmas 2002, Peter is back with his parents in Germany, experiencing severe heroin withdrawal.

Pages 100 – 101
A page written during Peter's first stint in prison, for burglary of Carl Barât's flat. Describing the different inmates whom he has shared his cell with, and his first appearance in the tabloid press.

Pages 102 – 103
At manager Alan McGee's house in Wales, reunited with Carl, attempting to write some songs together. During this time, Carl smashed his face up on a bathroom sink and damaged his eye.

Pages 105 – 106
Recalling a recent Libertines gig at the infamous Rhythm Factory without bass player John.

Pages 110 – 111
Lyrics to early song 'Lust of the Libertines'.

Pages 118 – 119
Feelings of bitterness, betrayal and hatred towards Carl and the Libertines, following being kicked out of his band, summer 2004.

Page 120
This book is from autumn 2004; Babyshambles are now a proper outfit, garnering rave reviews from critics and fans.

Page 120 & Page 183
© Mirrorpix

Page 125
Explaining how events beyond Peter's control get out of hand, prior to a gig he is due to play for a friend/fan's birthday which he never turned up for, and how people arranging things for him i.e. his manager and roadie, without his consent confuses and frustrates him.

Page 127
© *Evening Standard*; photograph © Angela Lubrano/Livepix.

Page 132
Cuttings from on an article about Peter featured in *Move*, a Stoke on Trent, music fanzine. Reproduced with their kind permission.

Page 134
Photo of the police barrier holding back fans at Peter's solo appearance at the Love Music Hate Racism gig in Trafalgar Square.

Page 144 – 147
In a recording studio in Wales recording Babyshambles debut LP, *Down in Albion*. Spring 2005.

Page 146
Lyrics to an unreleased Babyshambles song 'Gang of Gin', about Peter's feelings of being kicked out of the Libertines, and his loathing of the music industry.

Page 150
A written account/letter to a hotel manager, where Peter, Kate Moss, Bobby Gillespie and his girlfriend Katie England are staying, detailing the smashing up of their hotel room.

Page 152
Following legal troubles with film maker Max Carlish, and other gathering problems surrounding his life and the band, Peter warns his manager, James Mullord, that it is such circumstances that lead him to run off and abandon such trivial matters.

Page 164
A page written by Kate Moss.

Page 171
An account of a trip to Paris for designer Hedi Slimane's birthday party, and events on the Eurostar back to England,

Page 182
Notes on a Babyshambles gig in Norway.

Pages 188, 190 – 191, 198 & 126
Reproduced with kind permission of the *Guardian/Observer Music Monthly.*

Page 189
A drawing of Peter surrounded by lyrics and names of his songs, given to him by a fan.

Pages 192 – 201
Various reports of the Babyshambles nineteen-date autumn 2005 tour.

Pages 199 & 231
Photography © Jamie-James Madina

Pages 202 – 203
A typical scene in Peter's flat, looking about the place for drugs, blood graffiti on the walls, and the goings on involving the various characters present.

Pages 207 – 208
Lyrics to 'Albion'. Words and music by Peter Doherty © 2005. Reproduced by permission of EMI Music Publishing Ltd/Rough Trade Music Ltd, London WC2H 0QY.

Page 209
Memories of smuggling girls into his bunk on an early Libertines tour, against the tour manager's instructions.

Page 215
Working out lyrics for 'Stone Me, What a Life', a song Peter has written about the life of Tony Hancock.

Page 219
Questioning the endless accusations and legal charges he constantly has to face, when all he wishes to do is write and sing songs.

Page 221
Lyrics to 'Raise the Kaboose'.

Page 222
Reproduced by kind permission of the *East London Advertiser.*

Page 227
Lyrics to 'A Fool There Was'.

Page 233
Forced to remain behind bars for a period prior to a court case, early 2006. Reflections on his actions, the past, the justice system, the law and prison.

Page 244
Photograph (bottom) © Sally Anchassi.

Pages 245 – 261
Photos from winter/spring 2006. Reproduced by kind permission of Alizé Meurisse.

Pages 262 – 269
Putting parts of his life into the form of a narrative, Peter will refer to a character form of himself under the name of Villein. This gives him the ability to describe his life, and the events that take place, and his thoughts and feelings in the form of fiction i.e a novel/story.

Page 270
Photograph reproduced by kind permission of *Musikexpress*.

Page 277
An open apology and explanation on Peter's non attendance at a Babyshambles gig in Dublin.

Page 280
Photograph reproduced by kind permission of Jeannie Rau.

Page 282
In an airport in Amsterdam, reflecting on photographs that have been published in tabloid newspapers apparently showing Peter 'injecting an unconscious girl' (the photo was actually a mock-up).

Pages 286 – 293
Another extract from a novel in progress.

Pages 294 – 295
Working out lyrics and verse for a version of 'Pranging Out (Pete's Version)', a single by Mike Skinner's The Streets. Words and music by Peter Doherty and Mike Skinner © 2006. Reproduced by permission of EMI Music Publishing/Rough Trade Music Ltd, London WC2H 0QY.

Page 297
'Venus In Furs'. Words and music by Lou Reed © 1967. Screen Gems – EMI Music Inc/Oakfield Avenue Music Ltd, USA. Reproduced by permission of Screen Gems – EMI Music Ltd, London WC2H 0QY.

Pages 298 – 299
A report of Peter and fellow Babyshambler Mick Whitnall's trip to Portugal to be fitted with anti-heroin implants.

Pages 304 – 313
In the 'potting shed' (Peter's retreat) in Kate's garden, reflecting on recent events and considering the future, and a drug-free existence.

Pages 314 – 320
Early 2007, in rehab, in London's Nightingale Clinic.

Cover
Self-portrait of Peter Doherty courtesy of James Allen & Bankrobber – www.bankrobberlondon.com

Book photography
Steve Double

Designer: Adam Shutler
Art Director: Lucie Stericker
Consultant Editor: Earl Broad
Commissioning Editor: Ian Preece

Peter Doherty quote in the prelims taken from *Pete Doherty: Last of the Rock Romantics* by Alex Hannaford, published by Ebury. Reprinted by permission of The Random House Group Ltd.

The publisher would like thank:
Peter, Andy Boyd and Adrian Hunter (of Lazy Eye Management), Gerry O' Boyle, Kate Moss, Earl Broad, Adam Shutler, Alizé Meurisse, Clara Mills and Richard Thomas.

First published in hardback in Great Britain in 2007 by
Orion Books
an imprint of the Orion Publishing Group Ltd
Orion House, 5 Upper St Martin's Lane,
London WC2H 9EA
An Hachette Livre UK Company

1 3 5 7 9 10 8 6 4 2

A CIP catalogue record for this book is available from the British Library.

ISBN: 978 0 7528 8591 9

Printed by Printer Trento Italy

www.orionbooks.co.uk

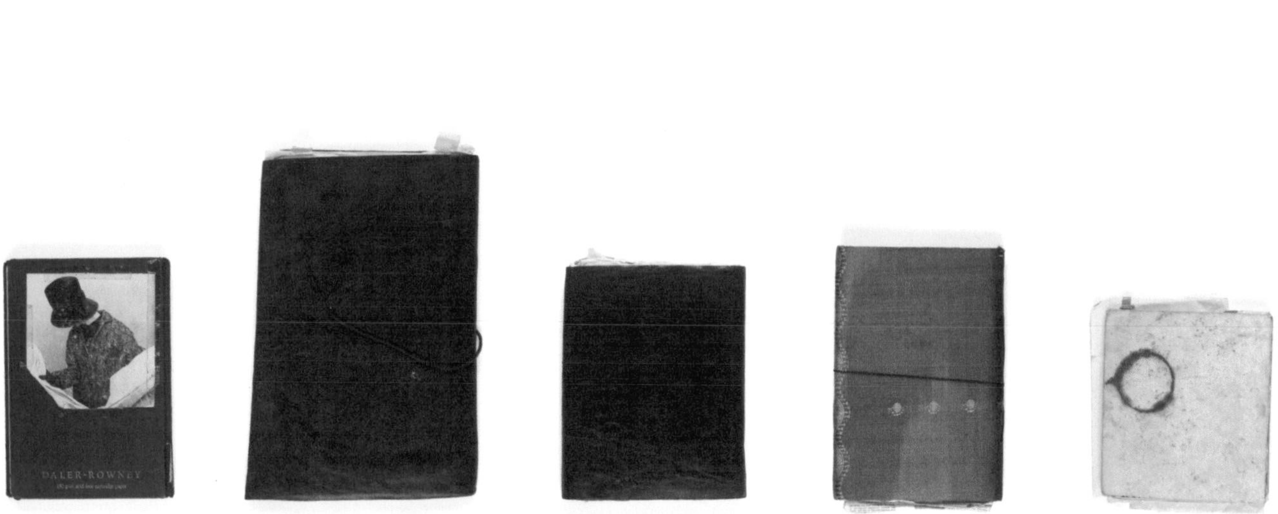
DALER-ROWNEY

DALER-ROWNEY
DALER-ROWNEY